I0176637

The Coming Deception

The Coming Deception

by Sylvia Bambola

Heritage Publishing House

Copyright © 2020 by Sylvia Bambola. All rights reserved. No part of this book may be used or reproduced in any manner whatsoever without written permission of the publisher.

For information contact:
Heritage Publishing House
heritagepubhouse@gmail.com

ISBN: 978-0-9657389-2-7

Unless otherwise indicated, all Scriptures taken from Holy Bible, King James version, Cambridge, 1769

Also by Sylvia Bambola

Non-Fiction
12 Questions New Christians Frequently Ask
Following the Blood Trail from Genesis to Revelation

Fiction:
Mercy at Midnight
The Babel Conspiracy
The Daughters of Jim Farrell
The Salt Covenants
Rebekah's Treasure
Return to Appleton
Waters of Marah
Tears in a Bottle
Refiner's Fire

To
My Children and Grandchildren
With Love

Table of Contents

Introduction

The Coming Deception isn't a "feel good" book or a book about how to be happier or more successful or be a better you. In fact, this book may make some angry and others question their theology. Though writing a book like *The Coming Deception* may cause controversy that was not my intention. Rather, writing it was born out of love for the body of Christ and love for God's Word. There is not enough teaching on this topic and consequently we have left many in the church as well as our children and grandchildren unprepared for what is coming down the pike. Hosea 4:6 says, *"my people are destroyed for lack of knowledge."* Knowledge is indeed power. And the information contained in this book is a forewarning of the coming dangers.

After Satan's rebellion and subsequent punishment, he remained obsessed with "becoming like god." This has manifested through a vindictive desire to destroy God's creation, including mankind, and a perverse desire to recreate man in his image. Because of this, many, like sheep, have been led to the proverbial slaughter, physically and spiritually.

I praise God for those who read this book and find value in it. For those who don't, I ask only one thing, that you take this information to God and allow Him to confirm or deny it.

When Jesus spoke about the signs of the end times in Luke 12:8, the first thing He mentioned was deception. *"Take heed that ye be not deceived."* May God and His wisdom prepare us for the **coming deception**.

The Cosmic War Begins

This battle is ancient and raged long before Adam and Eve walked beneath the cool shade of an incredible garden of delights. It's a battle that has played out for millennia and found its way into Paradise itself; a battle that eventually sucked our first parents into its vortex though they were hardly innocent victims. It's a battle that has affected us throughout history and continues affecting us today.

Understanding the depth of what's coming next requires understanding the past. Some may wonder why it even matters. The past is the past. It can't be changed. Ah, but it does matter. It matters because history repeats itself. Solomon said in Ecclesiastes 1:9, *"The thing that hath been, it is that which shall be; and that which is done is that which shall be done: and there is no new thing under the sun."* He's saying that what's happened in the past is going to happen again. It's a cycle, a circle of events that is repeated. And it's at our door.

It's a battle between God and Satan, between good and evil, and we are in the crossfire. How do we know there is an angel war? Daniel 10:12-13 gives us a clue. Daniel prayed and fasted and sought God after he had received a prophecy he didn't understand. For twenty one days he waited for the answer and when it came via God's messenger, Daniel was told the reason it took so long was because the prince of Persia (the ruling demonic spirit over Persia) prevented the messenger from coming and that Michael, a chief prince/angel, had to assist him.

Satan and his cohorts are still trying to thwart us at every turn, especially when it comes to the things of God. The war is real. And it has real casualties. So, let's see how it all began.

God starts the clock.

Genesis 1:1 states, *"In the **beginning** God **created** the **heaven** and the earth."* The Hebrew word here for beginning is *reshiyth* and means the first or best of a group, the beginning of a series. Also, that word "created" in Genesis 1:1 is *bara* and means to create, to make something new, something that never existed before. God created a life-sustaining earth and neighboring planets that never existed before and it must have been wonderful, because God only creates the wonderful.

Then notice that word "heaven" is singular. In 2 Corinthians 12:2, Paul talks about being *"caught up to the third heaven"* into Paradise, indicating there is more than one heaven, more than one dimension. While eternity already existed in Genesis 1:1 as did God's abode—His dwelling place in the third heaven—this heaven was something new. This heaven, created in the beginning of a specific series, was our atmosphere and surrounding planetary bodies.

Yet the very next verse in Genesis 1:2 says, *"and the earth was **without form and void**, and **darkness** was upon the face of the deep."* The Hebrew words *"without form and void"* are *tohuw* and *bohuw*, and literally mean a desolation, a waste, a worthless thing. But aside from *tohuw* and *bohuw* used here in Genesis 1:2 these words are only used together twice more in the Bible: Isaiah 34:11 and Jeremiah 4:23. In both cases they explicitly refer to God's judgment.

Next, that word "darkness" in *"and darkness was upon the face of the deep"* gives us an even clearer picture. That word in Hebrew is *choshe* and means darkness, misery, destruction, wickedness. So, something happened between verse one and two of Genesis; something evil that caused the destruction and desolation of the earth, making it a worthless thing.

15

And finally, looking at the Hebrew word "was" in the sentence *"and the earth was without form and void"* is *hayah.* It's in the pluperfect tense indicating a past action. So, the more accurate translation would be, "the earth **became** without form and void." Or another way of saying it could be, "the earth was without form and void because it became that way."

Furthermore, God Himself tells us something important about creation in Isaiah 45:18. *"For thus saith the Lord that created the heavens, God himself that formed the earth and made it; he that established it, he created it **not in vain**, he formed it to be **inhabited**; I am the Lord and there is none else."*

That word "vain" is *tohuw.* It's the same word and meaning used in Genesis 1:2, "a desolation, to lay waste, a worthless thing."

So, what is God saying here? He's saying He's the creator. He made it all. There's no one else. And He didn't create it *tohuw.* He didn't create it a waste, a desolation or a worthless thing. Rather, He created it to be inhabited, again indicating that something terrible happened between Genesis 1:1 and 1:2.

Even Jeremiah 4:23-27 tells us that before the earth was destroyed it was fruitful and had life as well as cities. *"I beheld the earth, and lo, it was **without form*** *and void, and the heavens and they had no light. I beheld the mountains, and lo, they trembled, and all the hills moved lightly. I beheld and lo, there was no man* (indicating this was before the creation of man) *and all the birds of the heavens were fled.* **I beheld and lo, the fruitful place was a wilderness and all the cities thereof were broken down at the presence of the Lord and by his fierce anger.** *For thus hath the Lord said, the whole land shall be desolate, yet will I not make a full end."*

As mentioned before, those words in Jeremiah 4:23-27, *"without form and void"* are *tohuw* and *bohuw* and clearly denote destruction. Just prior to this, God tells Jeremiah He is angry with Judah for their wickedness. At that time, the twelve tribes were split into two groups. The ten northern tribes were called Israel. The two southern tribes were called Judah. It is to these two southern tribes, to Judah, that God directs this prophesy, and foretells what He plans to do. But the prophesy is in the form of a vision of what happened in Genesis 1:2 to make the earth *"without form and void,"* indicating that He is going to do this same thing to Judah. So, God is using something that has already happened to illustrate what is going to happen.

Jeremiah's vision not only indicates there was life on earth before the creation of man but that God, in His fierce anger, partially destroyed it. But He didn't destroy it completely, just like He wouldn't completely destroy Judah.

It amazes me that the earth had cities. That word "cities" in Hebrew is *ayar* and means a city. But it also means a settlement or a place guarded by a watchman. And in these cities, settlements or places there was even a Garden of Eden, as we will see.

We can only imagine what those cities were like. They must have been stunningly beautiful. Everything must have flowed in perfect harmony. And Satan seems to have overseen it all. God, in Ezekiel 28:13-19 describes him as the *"anointed cherub that **covereth**."* That word "covereth" is *sakak* and means a cover, a hedge, defend, defense, which is what a watchman does. He keeps watch over a certain place to protect it, to defend, to cover it as a hedge of protection. Remember, that's one of the definitions of "cities," a place protected or guarded by a watchman.

And in Ezekiel 28:13-14, God tells us that Satan, as an exalted cherub, had *"been in Eden the garden of God, every precious stone was thy covering, the sardius, topaz, and the diamond, the beryl, the onyx, and the jasper, the sapphire, the emerald, and the carbuncle, and gold: the workmanship of thy tabrets and of thy pipes was prepared in thee in the day that thou was created."*

What a creature Satan must have been before the fall! He wore nine of the twelve precious stones sewn onto the ephod of Israel's high priest (Exodus 28:17). It seems that among Satan's other duties, he operated in some priestly capacity. At any rate, the angelic civilizations must have been beautiful and opulent indeed! And since Satan was the watchman in charge before his fall, it may explain why he was still hanging around the Garden of Eden after the six days of creation.

We need to understand there was a vast amount of time between verse one and verse two of Genesis. How long? We can't know. But it seems there was a thriving angelic civilization inhabiting the earth and the surrounding planetary bodies. And, as a high-ranking angel, Satan was a vital part of it.

Ok, but is there anything that points to an actual angelic civilization?

Paul reminds us that we see through a glass darkly (1 Corinthians 13:12) and so the best we can do is piece together the scant clues available, while understanding it's sketchy and subject to change as more clues are uncovered.

We'll begin with the Kings List. It was found by Hermann Hilprecht, a German American scholar in 1906. A stone table, at least four thousand years old and inscribed with Sumerian cuneiform writing, it lists a total of 143 kings that ruled the land. But here's the interesting part: the first eight kings mentioned were said to have "descended from heaven" and ruled for a combined total of 241,200 years![1]

These were not mere mortals. No eight men on earth ever lived those combined years. They had to be angelic beings. But how would the Sumerians know about them if they reigned before the six days of creation? Easy, through knowledge given them by angels when they began interacting with man after Adam and Eve were expelled from the garden. More about that in the next chapter.

Many myths and legends speak of advanced civilizations prior to the flood. Webster defines a myth as, "a traditional story of unknown authorship, ostensibly with a historical basis, but serving usually to explain some phenomenon of nature, the origin of man, or the customs, institutions, religious rites, etcetera, of a people." And Webster defines a legend as, "a story of some wonderful event, handed down for generations among a people and popularly believed to have a historical basis, although not verifiable."

So, let's look at a few.

One such legend is Atlantis, which Plato made famous in 360 B.C. He wrote it as fiction but claimed it was based on information passed down by a priest of Sais.[2] It appears that 200 years earlier, Solon, a Greek legislator, heard this story from the Egyptian priest, Sonchis of Sais, who said it was factual.[3]

Atlantis boasted of advance technology, was populated by demi-gods, was incredibly powerful and matchless in war. But pride and corruption brought them to an end. It mirrors, in many ways, the account of the Genesis angels cohabitating with woman and producing hybrid giants prior to the flood. Interestingly, the legend of Atlantis will have far reaching consequences, impacting even our current time.

Though the description of Atlantis falls more perfectly in a pre-flood timeline rather than pre-Adamic, it still shows a civilization far superior to that of a human one and, while considered myth or legend, may have clues into what a real angelic civilization could have been like.

Another myth is Lemuria, believed to be even older than Atlantis and which has caught the attention of occultists and New Agers.[4] Even evolutionists use Lemuria as the reason no one can find missing links to prove Darwin was right. They claim that Lemuria was the very place where evolution took place and since it sank into the sea, there's no way of retrieving this proof. Pretty convenient!

But other myths of mysterious and advanced civilizations abound. Here are a few: Khembolung (a utopian paradise found in Tibetan scriptures),[5] Avalon (Arthurian legendary island based on *Historia Regum Britanniae*, a pseudo-history written in 1136),[6] Buyan (Slavic mythical island which can disappear and reappear),[7] Kitezh (mystical city said to lay beneath Lake Svetloyar in Russia. Objects found by archaeologists in 2011 are believed to be associated with this city).[8] From these myths or legends we can envision, though poorly, how advanced the angelic civilization was and that it did not conform to natural laws.

A look at another ancient epic, one from India called the Mahabharata, written around 400 B.C.[9] reveals something startling. This epic describes flying machines called Vimana and lists the materials needed to construct one. Operating instructions as well as the Vimana's destructive capabilities, are also included.[10] Below is an excerpt.

"Strong and durable must the body of the Vimana be made, like a great flying bird of light material. Inside one must put the mercury engine with its iron heating apparatus underneath. By means of the power latent in the mercury which sets the driving whirlwind in motion, a man sitting inside may travel a great distance in the sky. The movements of the Vimana are such that it can vertically ascend, vertically descent, move slanting forwards or backward. With the help of the machines, human beings can fly in the air, and heavenly beings can come down to earth."[11]

The Vimana was also described in other ancient materials such as the Rigveda (Sanskrit text written around 1500 B.C),[12] Samarangana Sutradhara (Sanskrit text on ancient architecture), Yajurveda, and Ramayana (both ancient Sanskrit texts).[13]

In addition, the Law of the Babylonians says that, *"the privilege of operating a flying machine is great. The knowledge of flight is among the most ancient of our inheritances. A gift from those from upon high. We received it from them as means of saving many lives."*[14]

It's clear that man had forbidden knowledge given them by others, knowledge first used in a pre-

Adamic world. Some proofs of this are the OOParts, the out of place artifacts found by archaeologists. Perhaps the most famous is the ancient analogue computer, the Antikythera mechanism, which can track solar and lunar eclipses. It was found in the waters off the coast of Antikythera Island and believed to date anywhere from 205 B.C. to 87 B.C.[15]

And what about the ancient Sumerian cylinder seals detailing extensive knowledge of the solar system, including Pluto which wasn't even "discovered" until 1930?[16]

In 1999, Scientists at Bashkir State University in Russia discovered a map carved into a monolith of dolomite and diopside glass. When analyzed, they found that "the map was aligned with the magnetic north of 120 million years ago."[17]

Ley lines and grids also tell a story. Wikipedia defines ley lines as "straight alignments drawn between various historic structures and prominent landmarks." And the Free Dictionary defines a grid as, "a term used in giving the location of a geographic point by grid coordinates." Essentially, these networks transverse the earth and intersect at various localities. It's where resonating energy was discovered during various experiments. Many megaliths, henges, mounds and pyramids are situated along their intersections, including the Pyramids of Giza, Puma Punku, Machu Picchu, Easter Island, the Bermuda Triangle, and the Nazca Lines. The fact that they are so precisely linked indicates knowledge beyond even what today's modern science possesses.[18]

In addition, the earth is littered with signs that master builders have once worked here. Baalbek is perhaps one of the best examples. An ancient site located in the Beqaa Valley in Lebanon, the ruins of temples are still visible. Worshipers of Bacchus and Jupiter once thronged its streets. But beneath that area lay ruins of uncertain origin, dating to at least the Neolithic period or 12,000 years ago.

Recently, a team from the German Archaeological Institute uncovered at Baalbek what many believe is the largest ancient block in the world. It measures 64 feet by 20 feet by 18 feet. That's almost as long as five SUVs lined up front to back. And the block weighs in at a whopping 1,820 tons![19] A fully grown African bush elephant weighs about 6.5 tons. That means the weight of this block is equal to the weight of 280 elephants!

If the dating of the stone is correct, then it predates Adam since most Bible scholars believe, based on Biblical genealogies, that Adam was created about

6,000 years ago. But whether the date of the Baalbek stone is correct or not, it illustrates that mere men could not create or move such a structure, and hints at the type and scale of what an angelic civilization could be like.

Finally, we look outward, to Mars. A huge sphynx-like face was photographed in 1976 by the Viking Mars probe, along with a cluster of pyramid-like objects in what NASA calls the Cydonia region of Mars. It's interesting to note that the most accurate translation in Greek for "pyramid" is "the mound of Mars."[20]

The face and pyramids have been investigated for years. In 1997, NASA was visited by representatives of thirty independent scientists requesting permission to see the images, when available, of the Cydonia area, those taken by the Mars Global Surveyor spacecraft. The craft, launched in 1996, began its primary mapping mission in 1999, and mapped Mars for over nine years until its battery failed.[21] When the scientists reviewed the images, many, who had previously been skeptical, came to the conclusion that the "Cydonia Face (which measures 1.5 miles long, 1,500 feet high and 1.2 miles wide)[22] had to be an artificial structure,"[23] meaning it wasn't part of the natural landscape. In other words, someone constructed it!

In addition, giant geoglyphs, like those on the Nazca desert in Peru, were observed on Mars. Scientists also observed "huge glassy tubes" that extend for hundreds of miles. Dr. Tom Van Flandern, astronomer with a Ph.D. from Yale and former consultant to the Army Research Laboratory in Maryland before his death in 2009, described the tubes this way:

"White bands wrap around the tube about every ten meters along its entire length. The material between bands is translucent, and we can faintly see the white bands on the underside through the tube . . . In some places, they (the tubes) can be traced underground in infrared images that can detect such things if they are not too far below the surface . . . In a few places, many tubes come together in patterns suggestive of 'terminals' for train stations."[24]

It's easy to imagine angels floating among the clouds, above it all. It's much harder to imagine them eating or building things or using the common and familiar items we use such as chairs and books. But that's exactly what they did and do. John, in Revelation 4:1-4, was taken up to heaven where he saw a throne and God sitting on it. He also saw twenty-four seats and twenty-four elders who sat on them, elders who wore "white raiment" and had gold "crowns" on their heads. That means there was a literal throne and God was literally sitting on it. And there were twenty-four chairs with elders sitting on them, elders who wore clothes and crowns.

In addition, Revelation 21:27 talks about the Lamb's Book of Life. There are other books mentioned in the Bible such as the Book of Remembrance (Malachi 3:16) and a book about each of us and our life as indicated by Psalms 139:16. Also, Daniel 7:10 tells us there is a court in heaven where these books are opened. There is even a book about nations as mentioned in Revelation 10:8-11. If there are so many books, the natural conclusion is that there must also be a library in which to house them.

Revelation 11:19 also tells us there is a temple in heaven and an ark. So, in just these few scriptures we see that there are chairs, clothes, crowns, a temple, a throne, a library and books in heaven. It's not just a vapory environment. Heaven is an actual place where angels and the people of God use real, tangible items.

In John 13:2, Jesus said that in His Father's house were many mansions and that He was going back to prepare a place for us. Therefore, we can conclude there are other buildings in heaven, too, homes, dwellings, places to live.

Because heaven is a tangible place, it shouldn't be difficult to believe that angels built things on earth. Doesn't the Bible tell us that New Jerusalem, the heavenly city, will be made of gold, with walls of jasper and gates of pearls? (Revelation 21:2, 10-21) Hardly a thing of vapor!

The Bible allows us to see angels in relatable ways. When Elijah's servant, in 2 Kings 6:15-17, became frightened after seeing the Syrian army surrounding him, Elijah prayed that God would open his eyes to see the real picture. And when God did, the servant saw an angelic army in chariots that far outnumbered the Syrian's.

And didn't Abraham entertain God (Who was Jesus preincarnate) and two angels, and served them a meal of beef and cakes? (Genesis 18:1-8) Yes, angels can look like men and they do eat. Psalms 78:24-25 tells us that the manna given to the Israelites during their forty-years of wandering was "angels' food."

So, we see that these angelic beings do many of the things we do. They build and utilize structures, use books, eat and drive vehicles. And of course, they do many things we cannot.

From the few clues noted above, our take-away can easily be that our history books are incomplete. Our earth and probably other planetary bodies were populated, at one time, by angels who created a sophisticated and highly advanced society until something went horribly wrong.

The downfall and destruction

So, what happened between Genesis 1:1 and 1:2? A rebellion! A rebellion of unimaginable scope that disrupted God's perfect order. Satan became impressed with himself. He began to believe he would make a better god than God. He declared his evil intention in his five "I wills" found in Isaiah 14:13-14. These passages detail how this created being had the audacity to think he could usurp God, the Creator of all.

"For thou (Lucifer) *has said in thine heart, I will ascend into heaven, I will exalt my throne above the stars of God: I will sit also upon the mount of the congregation in the sides of the north: I will ascend above the heights of the clouds; I will be like the most High."*

Here in Isaiah, Satan said he would ascend into heaven, suggesting that he wasn't in heaven at the time, probably because he was ruling on earth and possibly the galaxy as well. But that wasn't enough for him. He wasn't content governing a vast empire and officiating as priest of the Most High. He wanted more. He wanted to be god. And that was his downfall—his delusions of grandeur.

But to begin his coup, the traitor had to spread discord by making accusations against God. The Bible doesn't tell us what he said. We can only image the evil lies he made up about God's character, His motives, perhaps even His fitness and right to rule. But whatever was said, it had to be convincing enough to cause one-third of all the angels to join the insurrection.

I suppose Satan believed this was only a start; that other angels might defect and follow him, too. Even so, he must have believed that he and his present band of cohorts were enough to successfully thwart God's authority and power. But whatever his thoughts, the battle lines were now drawn.

So, what was God to do?

He could have clamped the rebels in irons and cast them into the deepest pit, never to be seen or heard from again. After all, they were created beings. *His* created beings. But that could leave Satan's lingering accusations to possibly foment another rebellion among those angels still loyal.

It was a predicament.

How was God to once and for all illustrate His true loving character and lay to rest all the lies and accusations perpetuated by Satan? And how was He to exert His authority and justice while, at the same time, allowing Satan to expose *his* true nature?

Since God knows the beginning from the end and everything in between, He knew what it would take to fully restore His kingdom. And He knew it would come at great cost.

God's plan was brilliant, magnanimous, and terrifying all at once. He would create a dimension called time, containing a set span of seconds, minutes, hours, days, months, years in which He would unfold His plan and display His true nature while exposing Satan's, and thus repair the torn fabric of His kingdom.

God begins by declaring His own five "I Wills," and one "will I," pronouncing Satan's fate in Ezekiel 28:16-18, the fullness of which will not occur until after Jesus' thousand-year reign. *"I* (God) *will cast thee* (Satan) *as profane out of the mountain of God: and I will destroy thee, O covering cherub, from the midst of the stones of fire . . . I will cast thee to the ground, I will lay thee before kings, that they may behold thee. . .therefore will I bring forth a fire from the midst of thee,* *it shall devour thee, and **I will** bring thee to ashes upon the earth in the sight of all them that behold thee."*

God was telling Satan you're fired! From your exalted position I will reduce you to nothing, and everyone will see it! All of Satan's empire would be cast to the ground, become dust, worthless. And all those who ruled with him would see his demise. And so, the destruction of Satan's kingdom on earth and elsewhere commenced.

Though God doesn't imprison or destroy Satan, justice demanded a penalty be paid. Rebellion of that magnitude could not go unpunished. To begin, Satan would lose his exalted status. According to Job 1:6-12, he was still allowed to "present" himself before the Lord and assemble with the other angels, but he was no longer that glittering bejeweled cherub. How this must have irked him! You can see it in his character when he slanders Job, accusing him of wrong motives for serving God. And how happy he must have been when God gave him permission to hurt Job and his family and property. Only Job's life was out of bounds.

What a contrast to the powerful cherub who sang praises before God and supervised His creation. Now, a sniveling accuser, a spreader of lies, his primary activity was hurting the things God loved.

But there was more to the punishment. It involved the destruction of earth and other planetary bodies, along with all of Satan's holdings on them. The marvelous civilization Satan had helped set up would now be ground into dirt. God would make it *tohuw*. He would make it all a worthless thing.

Again, rereading Jeremiah 4:23-27 we see what God did. *"I beheld the earth, and lo, it was without form and void; and the heavens and they had no light. I beheld the mountains, and lo, they trembled, and all the hills moved lightly. I beheld and lo, there was no man* (indicating this was before the creation of man) *and all the birds of the heavens were fled.* **I beheld and lo, the fruitful place was a wilderness and all the cities thereof were broken down at the presence of the Lord and by his fierce anger.** *For thus hath the Lord said,* **the whole land shall be desolate, yet will I not make a full end.**"

Many Bible scholars believe this is when the first earth was destroyed as God rendered a partial judgment.

These same Bible scholars believe there is a literal gap between Genesis 1:1 and Genesis 1:2, and call it the Gap Theory. They believe that God, beginning in Genesis 1:3, was restoring the original earth rather than creating it. And, yes, I believe that the six days of creation/restoration were six literal days.

To further back up the Gap Theory, Genesis 1:28 in the King James Bible tells us that after God created man, He gave him the charge to not only be fruitful and multiply by having children, but to *replenish* the earth.

According to *Webster's New World Dictionary* plenish means to fill up, stock, while replenish means to **fill again**. Here the Hebrew word for replenish is *mala* and is the exact word used when God, in Genesis 9:1, commands Noah to *replenish* the earth after the flood destroys everything. So, twice God commands man to replenish the earth, the first time in the garden, the second time after the flood. He's telling them to restore the land, to cultivate the soil and plant, to make the earth flourish again.

Some scientific evidence, such as carbon dating, fossil records, and the age of certain rock formations, suggest this is an old earth. While other evidence, like the oldest reef—the Great Barrier Reef—being less than 5,000 years old, the earth's slowing rotation, and the declining magnetic field, all point to a young earth. Based on the Gap Theory, we can understand how both can be true. There is no contradiction.

But is there any evidence of this destruction?

Yes.

Geological evidence supports that the earth was bombarded thousands of years ago, though some say millions. As a result of this bombardment, iridium deposits are found in earth's K-T layer[25] -- the sediment that differentiates geologically between the Cretaceous and Tertiary periods which translates roughly to the dinosaur age. Accurate dating is an ongoing issue between scientists. While one group will look at a body of evidence and say it represents "millions" of years, others will look at the same evidence and claim it is only "thousands" of years. And when fossil tracks of man-like creatures and dinosaurs were found together in a Texas river-bed and elsewhere, it only added to the confusion.[26]

Archeological dating methods, such as carbon dating, rather than being an exact science is one of interpretation and accounts for how and why so many scientists disagree and can come up with very different conclusions. Nevertheless, it's rare to find iridium on earth, especially in the quantities found in the K-T layer. But it's readily found in asteroids and comets. This layer, which is deep beneath the surface, and comprised of clay and ash, is found on every land mass on earth indicating a catastrophic global bombardment.[27]

Author Bryant Stavely describes the layer this way: *"And within this ash and clay are a preponderance of . . . tektites, shocked quartz, and/or glassy gobules of fused sand/dirt, the kind of which are produced by the intense heat of either a meteor strike, or a nuclear detonation . . . and many of them are slightly radioactive still."*[28]

In addition, our moon is cratered and scarred as a result of several destructive impacts. Mars did not escape either. The blows to it were so severe they caused a polar shift, along with deep cratering and scorching on one side.[29] Some scientists believe that the vast quantity of existing space debris is the result of what happened during this time.

Along with the earth, moon and Mars, it appears that Venus and Mercury were also damaged. They all appear to have sustained stress fractures that created ridges on their surface. Axis's were shifted. The destruction was cataclysmic and far reaching. In addition, Pluto, Neptune and Uranus' orbits were also affected. While Venus' was totally reversed.[30]

Conclusion:

Satan, the rebel, was now displaced. No longer a bigwig in heaven and no longer the overseer of a thriving angelic civilization, what was he to do? One thing was certain, he wasn't about to go quietly. Then, when God created Adam and Eve, he saw an opportunity not only for elevation but revenge. We know he was already a fallen angel when we first see him in the Garden of Eden tempting Eve because he came to her in the form of a serpent, making him a deceiver. And he lied to her, making him a liar. But this was all-out war. He needed to prove to his followers that he, not God, deserved to rule.

Probably to Satan's mind it wouldn't be difficult. Chances are he viewed God's new man-creatures as gullible and weak, inferior to him and his minions, surely easy prey. It had to be infuriating to have God give such a puny being dominion over the very earth he had once ruled. Since Satan's focus now was hurting, or better still, destroying the things God loved, that would be his way of comeback. If he could corrupt man, use him as a pawn in his war, then that would be a triumph indeed!

Ye Shall be as Gods

Was it easier than he thought, Satan's corruption of man with a lie? Perhaps. But it was the woman who was fooled first. He must have thought she would be the easier target because he waited until she was alone to spring his trap.

"Has God said Ye shall not eat of every tree of the garden?" he whispered, coiling his body around the trunk of the tree.

She seemed undisturbed by his presence and quickly answered that she and her husband could eat from every tree except the one *"in the midst of the garden."* Then she made a mistake. She told him God had said if they ate of it or **touched it** they would die. She was on shaky ground now. Satan knew God never told her she couldn't touch the tree or its fruits, only that she couldn't eat it. And that's all it took, just a sliver, the tiniest of openings, to get her to question what else God had said.

"Ye shall not surely die," Satan hissed. *"For God doth know that in the day ye eat thereof, then your eyes shall*

be opened, and ye shall be as gods, knowing good and evil."

And so it began, the beginning of the end. Eve partook, then her husband. And after they did, Genesis 3:7 tells us, *"And the eyes of them both were opened, and they knew that they were naked; and they sewed fig leaves together, and made themselves aprons."*

That word "naked" in Hebrew means "to make bare, to be cunning, to be crafty." In other words, Adam and Eve didn't just realize they weren't wearing clothes, they saw their craftiness. They had lost their innocence. And what a loss it must have been! Then, to cover up their craftiness, their nakedness, their exposed sin, they sewed fig leaves together.

From beautiful, holy beings clothed with the glory of God, Adam and Eve, the would-be-gods, were now covered with withering fig leaves.

It's interesting to note that the word "aprons" in Hebrew means "a belt, girdle, armor." But it also means to be afraid. So, Adam and Eve, afraid of what God would do when He saw their sin, their craftiness exposed, tried to cover it up. And from that time to this, man is still trying to cover up his sins by means of his own handiwork, his own solutions, his own good works. Every religion, except Christianity, tries to show man how to work his way back to God; how to sew aprons. While only Christianity shows how God made His way back to man.

God doesn't want aprons.

His requirement is very different. After Adam and Eve sinned, Genesis 3:21 tells us that, *"Unto Adam also and to his wife did the Lord God make coats of skins, and clothed them."*

But where did God get these coats? The first mention of innocent blood being shed in Scripture is here, by the hand of God, when He killed an animal in order to cover Adam and Eve, thus establishing from the very beginning, in Genesis, the criteria for covering sin: innocent blood.

God created man knowing Satan would continue fomenting rebellion, and knowing that man, too, would rebel. There are protocols in heaven that God won't break, spiritual laws He won't violate. And, according to Daniel 7:10 there is a heavenly court where books are opened, and judgments made. So, when Adam and Eve sinned it required a legal rendering. Judgment was pronounced. The first couple would lose dominion over the earth, the dominion God had given them. And that dominion was then legally transferred back to Satan.

He was in charge now, back in control, or at least partial control. That's why Jesus, in both John 12:31 and John 16:11, called Satan, *"the prince of this world"* and 2 Corinthians 4:4 calls Satan, *"the god of this world."* And that's why, in Matthew 4:8-10, Jesus didn't contradict Satan when the rebel promised to give Him all the kingdoms of the world if only He'd bow down to him. Jesus knew that due to Adam's sin, Satan had obtained the legal right to these kingdoms.

But Adam and Eve's sin didn't take God by surprise. John the Baptist, in John 1:29, called Jesus, *"the Lamb of God which taketh away the sin of the world."* And Revelation 13:8 talks about the *"Lamb slain from the **foundation of the world**,"* showing God's foreknowledge not only of man's original sin but also of what His intended solution would be.

Though things looked bleak that day in the Garden, God had it all under control. But it would take time for things to play out in order to accomplish the full restoration of His entire creation. A timeline, during which the cosmic war would continue to its conclusion, was established. It would involve many battles. And though the final victory is destined to be God's, it will cost Him greatly. But in the end, both heaven and earth will be perfectly restored. And God's holy name and character will be upheld. Even so, it will leave a blood trail from one end of Scripture to the other. I cover this in my book, *Following the Blood Trail from Genesis to Revelation*.

Satan must have thought he was home free after Adam and Eve's fall. He was in charge again. The earth was his. But then God put a damper on things. The Most High had already told Satan He would destroy him. And He had already demolished every vestige of Satan's planetary holdings, the angelic civilizations that had taken eons to build. Now, Satan's latest offense, this latest spitting in God's face, prompted yet another harsh judgment.

Because Satan had come in the guise of a serpent or perhaps just possessed one, and corrupted God's new creation, God's contempt was evident. In His righteous anger, the Most High relegates the serpent, which would forever be associated with Satan, to a belly crawler. The serpent would now eat dust. It would be the lowest of the low, to mirror Satan who was also the lowest of the low in God's eyes. From the *"anointed cherub"* he was now as low as dirt.

We already saw in Ezekiel 28:16-18 how after Satan pronounced his five "I wills" God responded with His own "I wills" and decreed Satan's destruction. But in Genesis 3:15, God told Satan the means of that destruction. *"And I will put enmity* (hatred) *between thee and the woman, and between thy seed and her seed; it shall bruise thy head, and thou shalt bruise his heel."*

I wonder if Satan thought God blew it by giving away His game plan. Satan now had an advantage. He knew where the focus had to be—on the seed of the woman, the very woman who would become mother of mankind, the very woman he considered inferior, the very woman he had so easily deceived. It was to be **her** seed that caused his ruination. The mere fact that God would try to use such a puny vessel to defeat the once great cherub must have irritated Satan. But thanks to God tipping His hand, Satan now had a chance to thwart it.

We know the seed in Genesis 3:15 is Jesus Who crushed Satan's head when He died on the cross to redeem mankind. But it also talks about another seed, Satan's. In both cases "seed" is the same word *zera* and means, "fruit, plant, sowing-time, child, posterity, to conceive seed, to bear." It's the same word used in Genesis when God talked about the seed of trees, herbs, and man. In other words, it's a physical seed or the physical product of that seed.

According to the *Theological Wordbook of the Old Testament*, *zera* is used in only four ways:

> 1) Time of sowing as in "seed time and harvest"
> 2) The physical seed which is scattered
> 3) The seed as semen
> 4) The Seed as the offspring in the promised line of Abraham, Isaac, and Jacob[31]

I always thought the seed of Satan, in Genesis, meant Satan's spiritual offspring, those who don't accept Jesus. And I still believe that's true. But this scripture indicates a physical seed. Though the concept of Satan having a physical seed seems bizarre, it's exactly what he will use in his attempt to thwart God's verdict. If he could corrupt the seed of woman, he could prevent the Deliverer from coming to crush him. And when Cain was born, Satan jumped into action and inspired a murderous heart in the first product of the woman's seed, disqualifying Cain as the promised one. But as humans began populating the earth, it became impossible to corrupt them all. And since he didn't know which seed would give rise to the Deliverer, Satan needed to come up with a better plan, a plan capable of causing wholescale corruption.

Sylvia Bambola

The plan unfolds

In Genesis 6:1-4 we see that plan revealed. *"And it came to pass, when men began to multiply on the face of the earth, and daughters were born unto them, That the sons of God saw the daughters of men that they were fair; and they took them wives of all which they chose . . . There were giants in the earth in those days; and also after that, when the sons of God came in unto the daughters of men, and they bare children to them, the same became mighty men which were of old, men of renown."*

So, the *"sons of God,"* who were fallen angels, physically took women as wives and produced children. Really? Surely these *"sons of God"* refer to someone else.

No. Every reference to the *"sons of God"* in the Old Testament, with one exception, refers to angels. First, we'll look at the angel references.

Job 1:6 *"Now there was a day when the **sons of God** came to present themselves before the LORD, and Satan came also among them."* Job 2:1 repeats this. *"Again there was a day when the **sons of God** came to present themselves before the LORD, and Satan came also among them to present himself before the LORD."*

46

Then in Job 38:6-7 God says to Job, *"Whereupon are the foundations thereof fastened? Or who laid the corner stone thereof; When the morning stars sang together, and all the **sons of God** shouted for joy?"* God is talking about the angels witnessing the creation of the world and how they rejoiced. So, we see that these passages refer only to angels.

Now, the one exception. It's in Hosea 1:9-11. In verse 9, God tells Hosea to name his son, Loammi, as a sign that the Israelites were no longer His people and He was no longer their God. Yet in the very next verse, verse 10, God says, concerning Israel, *"Ye are the sons of the living God."* And verse 11 tells us it's talking about the restoration of Judah and Israel in the **last days**, in the days of Jezreel, when God *will* call them His sons—referring to the end times when God restores Israel. So, yes, in the last days, God will call Israel His sons.

But why in the New Testament are men called the *"sons of God"*? John 1:12 tells us. *"But as many as received him* (Jesus), *to them gave the power to become the sons of God, even to them that believe on his name."* So now those who believe in Jesus are called, *"sons of God."* But it's only because of Jesus that we are adopted into God's family and are called sons.

47

It's interesting that when Luke, in chapter 3:23-38, talks about the lineage of Jesus He ends up with Adam, and calls Adam, *"the son of God."* But that's after He said in Luke 3:6, *"And all flesh shall see the salvation of God."* Adam was not called the son of God in the Old Testament. He had to wait until Jesus came and died in order to be called a son, in order to have his position restored before God.

So, we see that fallen angels mated with women and created, what the Bible calls, the Nephilim. Some Christians have difficulty with the concept of angels having sex. They often cite Mark 12:25 where Jesus said we, like the angels in heaven, will not marry after we're resurrected. But notice, Jesus never said the angels were incapable of having sex, only that the angels didn't marry. And the reason **we** don't marry in heaven is because, as the bride of Christ, we are already married to Jesus.

These Nephilim in Genesis 6:1-4 are described as, "giants, mighty men, and men of renown." Breaking down the Hebrew words will give us a better understanding. "Giants" (*naphal/nephilim*) means, "the **fallen ones,** bully or tyrant." "Mighty" (*gibbor*) means, "powerful, warrior, tyrant and **to rise oneself up in arrogance and stand in God's face.**" And "men" (*enosh*) in "men of renown" means, "frail, feeble, sick, desperately wicked, mortal." While "renown" (*shem*) means, "to mark or brand."

Putting it together we get a picture of what these angelic offspring were like:
- they are the fallen ones
- they're powerful
- they act as bullies and tyrants
- they are arrogant and defy God
- but they are now mortal
- and as such are feeble, frail in contrast to their former state
- and it suggests that they are marked or branded by God

If this is so, if fallen angels really did come down to earth and cohabitate with women and produced offspring, was this a well-known event?

Yes. The ancient Israelites understood Genesis 6:1-4 to mean fallen angels and that their offspring were the giants. This was the prevailing belief. And this was believed up to and including Jesus' day as well as during the early years of the church.

Flavius Josephus wrote about this in his *Jewish Antiquities*, a history of the Jews. A 1st Century Jew, he was born 37 A.D. in Jerusalem. A priest in the royal Hasmonean line—the line of the Maccabees—

he fought against Rome during the Jewish rebellion. And he was an eyewitness to the destruction of Jerusalem in 70 A.D.

Here's what he said: *"For many angels of God coupled with women, and begat sons that proved unjust, and despisers of all that was good, on account of the confidence they had in their own strength: for the tradition is, that these men did what resembled the acts of those whom the Grecians call giants."*[32]

So, Josephus claims the so-called Greek mythology was based on these Nephilim. In other word, the Titans and Olympians were Nephilim, the offspring of fallen angels. And according to Genesis 6:4, this occurred twice. *"There were giants in the earth in those days; and **also after that**, when the sons of God came in unto the daughters of men, and they bare children to them, the same became mighty men which were of old, men of renown."*

So, we see this occurred before the flood as well as after.

Because the giants were hybrids, neither fully angelic nor fully human, they were an abomination to God. And when Israel entered the Promise Land, God ordered them to utterly destroy these giants. One such giant stronghold was Hebron. Here's what Josephus said about the Hebron massacre: *"When they* (the Israelites) *had taken it* (Hebron), *they slew all the inhabitants. There were till then left the race of giants, who had bodies so large and countenances so entirely different from other men, that they were amazing to the sight and terrible to the hearing. The bones of these men are still shown to this very day, unlike any credible relations of other men."* And bones of giants were displayed well into the first century much like a museum artifact.[33]

If that's true, what did the early church fathers say about it?

Around 96 A.D., Clement of Rome (Pope from 88 A.D. to 99 A.D.) wrote, *"The giants* (were) *men of immense bodies, whose bones of enormous size are still shown in certain places for confirmation of their existence."*[34]

But even long after Clement, the bones were still available for viewing as Tertullian (early Christian theologian) notes around 200 A.D., *"There are the carcasses of the giants of old time; it will be obvious enough that they are not absolutely decayed, for their bony frames are still extant."*[35]

Other church fathers also wrote about these giants, among them Justin Martyr (100–165 A.D., Christian teacher); Irenaeus (125-202 A.D., Greek cleric who combated heresy); Lactantius (250–325 A.D., early Christian author); and Ambrose (339–397 A.D., Archbishop of Milan in 4th Century).[36]

Saint Augustine gives an eye-witness account: *"I have seen, and not I alone, on the shore by Utica, so huge a molar tooth of a man, that were it cut up into small models of teeth like ours, it would seem enough to make a hundred of them. But this I should think had belonged to some giant; for beside that the bodies of all men were much larger than ours, the giants again far exceeded the rest."*[37]

Giants are even mentioned in the Apocrypha, like the *Book of Wisdom, The Book of Jasher* (an ancient text that was also mentioned by Joshua and Samuel in the Old Testament) and *Baruch*. And III Maccabees 2:4 says, *"It was thou (God) who didst destroy the former workers of unrighteousness, among whom were the giants, who trusted in their strength and hardihood, by covering them with a measureless flood."*[38]

Jasher claims these angels (which he calls judges and rulers) not only took wives by force, but even those who were already married. *Jasher* also said these angels comingled the seed of different animals, creating hybrids and corrupting the earth.[39] But it doesn't end there. Many clues suggest that angels also comingled their seed with animals to create chimeras. Cave drawings and petroglyphs of chimeras can be seen in nearly every ancient culture around the world, including America.

But by the 5th Century, the church was uncomfortable with the concept of angels comingling their seed with women and animals, and came up with the Sethite Theory, claiming it was really the godly sons of Seth that comingled with the evil daughters of Cain, and this without any Scripture to support it.[40]

Greek, Roman and Norse myths define giants as "primordial creatures."[41] But they are not the only ones with legends of giants. Literally every culture around the world has them, including the Hindus, Siamese, American Indians, and Mongols. Even Alexander the Great (356-323 B.C.) claimed to be "of the seed of the serpent."[42]

Homer, a Greek poet and historian, in 400 B.C. wrote, *"On the earth there once were giants."*

And Francis Schaeffer, famous Evangelic Christian theologian, philosopher and pastor, put it this way, *"More and more we are finding that mythology in general, though greatly contorted, very often has some historic base. And the interesting thing is that one myth*

*which occurs over and over again in many parts of the
world is that somewhere, a long time ago, supernatural
beings had sexual intercourse with natural women and
produced a special breed of people.*"[43]

The *Book of Enoch* also mentions giants. According to
Genesis 5:22, Enoch *"walked with God."* He was 365
years old when he was raptured, taken by God
without first dying. Since Adam was 622 years old
when Enoch was born and lived another 308 years,
it means for over 300 years Enoch had access to
Adam and his knowledge.

Considered Apocrypha and not sacred text by any
except the Ethiopian Orthodox Tewahedo Church
and Eritrean Orthodox Church, The *Book of Enoch* is
surrounded in controversy. It's thought by some to
be just what it says, an accounting by Enoch in 3273
B.C. of what he saw. And later, after Enoch's death,
it seems to include some of Noah's writings as well.
Therefore, many consider it trustworthy history.
Others believe it was written much later and is
heresy. Most believe a few sections were corrupted
between Noah and Moses' day. Nevertheless, it was
well known in Jewish religious texts (*Zohar* and
Targum of Jonathan) as well as by the early church.
Tertullian considered the book genuine, but that
referred only to 1 Enoch or the first Book of Enoch.
Church fathers as well as rabbis considered it

"recommended reading," and was quoted by both Irenaeus and Origen (184–253 A.D., Christian scholar).[44]

Though a passage in the *Book of Enoch*[45] was quoted almost word-for-word by Jude in Jude 1:14-15, the book itself was placed outside Christian Scripture as the 4th Century rolled around.[46] Then it seems to have disappeared. In 1956 it was found among the Dead Sea Scrolls.

The *Book of Enoch* contains accurate prophecy as well as contradictions. Though some parts of the book have been corrupted, there are many parts that are still considered authentic and of value. I refer to it now as just another source that can possibly give us more insight into what happened regarding the giants.

What does the *Book of Enoch* say?

It's interesting to note that it is addressed to the people who will be living during the Tribulation or end times. His opening words are:

"These are the words of the blessing of Enoch, to bless the elect and righteous, who will be living in the day of Tribulation, when all the wicked and godless will be destroyed. God opened the eyes of the righteous Enoch, so

that the angels could show him a vision of the Holy One in the heavens. From them I understood that the vision I saw was not for my generation, but for a far distant one. On the account of the elect, the great Holy One, the God of the world, will come forth from His dwelling and tread upon the earth, appearing with His host in the strength of His might from the heavens."[47]

Enoch then goes on to talk about the many things the angels showed him: the stars and constellations, the winds, the hail, etcetera. But in 1 Enoch 6:1-8[49] he talks about how two hundred angels descended on Mount Hermon during his father, Jared's, time and made a pact with each other to take human wives. From the union with these women came the giants. Interestingly, Mt. Hermon can be translated, "make accursed" or "devoted to destruction."[49] Naming it Mt. Hermon, indicates God not only put it under a curse, but issued a prophetic warning to these fallen angels regarding their fate. Even later it was an unholy site, the place where, over the years, thirty different temples were erected to pagan gods.[50]

1 Enoch 7:1-6 talks about how these angels not only cohabitated with women but corrupted them by teaching them forbidden knowledge, including sorcery, enchantments, and the use of roots and plants (probably some form of drugs). It also talks about how the offspring, the giants, turned to

cannibalism and "began to sin against birds, and beasts, and reptiles, and fish, and to devour one another's flesh and drink the blood."[51] As previously mentioned, this corruption of animals was also mentioned in the *Book of Jasher* 4:18.[52]

The Book of Giants, also found among the Dead Sea Scrolls and attributed to Enoch, mentions this corruption of animals as well, though it's only a fragment. It says, ". . . two hundred donkeys, two hundred asses, two hundred . . . rams of the flock, two hundred goats, two hundred beasts of the field from every animal, from every bird . . . for **miscegenation** (interbreeding)" 1Q23 Frag. 1 +6.[53] This is outright sin against God who said in Genesis that every living thing should produce *"after his kind."* Some ancient texts confirm this, including a Canaanite tablet that claims giants (worshiped as gods) not only mingled the species but also had sex with animals. Perhaps this is why Leviticus 20:15-16 forbids humans from defiling themselves in this way.

Then, in the next chapter of Enoch it talks about Azazel teaching men to make metal implements of war and women to beautify their eyes.[54] According to 1 Enoch 10:6, God then judges Azazel for leading the two hundred angels who cohabitated with women and taught them forbidden knowledge:

"And again the Lord said to Raphael (a holy angel): *Bind Azazel hand and foot, and cast him into the darkness: and make an opening in the desert, which is in Dudael, and cast him therein. And place upon him rough and jagged rocks, and cover him with darkness, and let him abide there for ever, and cover his face that he may not see light. And on the day of the great judgment he shall be cast into the fire. . .. The whole earth has been corrupted through the works that were taught by Azazel, so ascribe all these sins to him."*[55]

It's interesting that during the Day of Atonement, God ordered Moses in Leviticus 16:8, 10, 26, to take two goats. *"And Aaron shall cast lots upon the two goats; one lot for the LORD, and the other lot for the scapegoat."* The blood of the first goat was poured upon the mercy seat for the sins of the nation. The other goat, the scapegoat, was taken into the wilderness and, according to Jewish tradition, was pushed over a cliff into a rocky ravine. And that word "scapegoat" in Hebrew is *Azazel*.

We know that the blood on the mercy seat is a foreshadowing of Jesus' blood and forgiveness for mankind. But what does Azazel, the scapegoat, mean? The goat that is thrown over a cliff? And why the two? Does it indicate that for mankind there is forgiveness but for the angels who left their first estate there is none? Remember, Enoch said that

God assigned all sin to Azazel, meaning the sin of the fallen angels for leading man astray and for teaching man forbidden knowledge and the sins produced by that knowledge. It seems to be prophetic, indicating that these fallen angels will be consignment to a pit. It certainly corresponds to Jude 6 that said these angels are now chained in darkness.

Perhaps this mystery points directly to the cosmic war and the heavenly protocols that deal with God's handling of the fallen angels. For now, it seems that not only man's sins must be covered but also those of the fallen angels, until such time that all will be judged.

A side note regarding angels teaching forbidden knowledge to men: Otzi the Ice Man is an example. He's mummified and believed to be about 5,300 years old, which puts him solidly into a pre-flood timeframe. X-rays show he suffered from osteoarthrosis and had forty-seven tattoos on his back, legs and left wrist in the very spots that today are considered acupuncture points for that disease.[56]

Back to Enoch. At some point these angels must have become afraid that the cry of hurting humanity would reach the ears of God so they went to Enoch, because *"he walked with God,"* and asked him to plead with God to forgive them for their great sin. Enoch did and God sent His answer through messengers, which Enoch calls "holy ones" and "Watchers."

There would be no forgiveness.

1 Enoch 12:5-6, "(Enoch) *tell them* (the fallen angels who cohabited with women) *that they will not have peace nor forgiveness of sin, for they will not delight in their children. They will witness the slaughter of their beloved ones, and weep over the destruction of their children, even if they petition for all eternity they will not obtain mercy or peace.*"[57]

As previously mentioned, Jude 6 alludes to these angels and says, *"And the angels which kept not their first estate, but left their own habitation, he (God) hath reserved in everlasting chains under darkness unto the judgment of the great day."*

Ephesians 6:12 says, *"For we wrestle not against flesh and blood, but against principalities, against powers, against the rulers of the darkness of this world, against spiritual wickedness in high places."* This tells us that not all fallen angels are presently chained, only those who left their first estate.

It was a wild gamble, Satan's plan to corrupt the seed of women, but terrifyingly successful. So much of her "seed" had become hopelessly entwined with his.

As things became increasingly bleak, the holy angels, according to 1 Enoch 9:1-11,[58] grew worried. *"Then Michael, Gabriel, Raphael and Uriel looked down from heaven and saw all the bloodshed upon the earth by the extreme lawlessness. They said one to another, 'the earth is laid waste and the voice of all the dead cries up to the gate of heaven. The souls of men cry out to the holy ones of heaven saying, 'bring our cause before the Most High.' They said to the Lord, the King, 'Lord of lords, God of gods, and King of kings, the throne of Your glory endures throughout all the ages, and Your name is holy, glorious and blessed unto all the ages! You have made all things, and have power over all things, and You see all things; nothing is hidden from You. You see what Azazel has done, teaching unrighteousness on earth and revealing the eternal secrets concealed in heaven. Semyaza and those he has authority over have taught sorcery. And they have defiled themselves by sleeping with the daughters of men and revealed to those women these kinds of sins. These women have begotten giants, and by their children the whole earth has been filled with blood and unrighteousness. Now the souls of the dead are crying out to the gates of heaven because of the lawlessness which has taken place on the earth. You know all things before they come to pass. You allow this, but have not told us what we should do to the giants who are destroying Your creation."*[59]

The fact that God waited so long testifies to His longsuffering. But His answer finally comes. *"I will destroy man whom I have created from the face of the earth; both man, and beast, and the creeping thing, and the fowls of the air; for it repenteth me that I have made them."* (Genesis 6:7)

How it must have hurt God to see the sad state of His creation! And how the enormity of the required judgment must have weighed heavily on Him! But He had to act or there wouldn't be a pure seed of the woman left to crush Satan's head.

Genesis 6:6 says, *"And it repented the LORD that he had made man on the earth, and it **grieved him at his heart**."* Did He weep over what He had to do? I think so. Didn't Jesus weep over Jerusalem when He envisioned its destruction because of the Jews' rejection of Him? And Jesus said if you've seen me you've seen the Father (John 14:9). He also said that He and the Father were one (John 10:30).

So, despite a heavy heart, God instructs Noah to build an ark. Then judgment would come. And out of all human flesh, only eight would survive: Noah, the great grandson of Enoch, and Noah's three sons, Shem, Ham and Japheth, and their wives along with the animals God told Noah to take that were *"after their kind"* (Genesis 6:20).

Genesis 6:9 tells us that, *"Noah was a just man and perfect in his generations, and Noah walked with God."* It's interesting to note that word "perfect" in Hebrew is *tamiym* and means, "without blemish, complete, full, whole, undefiled, upright, healthy, **soundness of flesh.**" Though Noah was just and upright in the eyes of God, *tamiym* denotes physical, not spiritual, purity. It indicated his flesh was sound. He was 100% human. His DNA had not been corrupted.

In order to preserve the Messianic blood line, God had to wipe out all corrupt human flesh by sending a flood. At the same time, He wiped out all the animals the Nephilim had corrupted through crossbreeding. God would start over through Noah and his offspring and the animals on the ark.

The date of the flood, according to Biblical genealogies, is believed to be around 2452 B.C.[60] It is depicted in Tablet XI of the Gilgamesh Epic.[61] And it's an account described in virtually every culture. Of special interest is the ancient Chinese language which holds amazing references. "Boat" is a three-character word indicating "a vessel, eight, and mouth."[62] In addition, Chinese history indicates that "Lo-Ham begat Cusah and Mesay."[63] which is a reference from Genesis 10:6 to the sons of Ham which were Cush and Mizraim (but also Phut and Canaan which are not mentioned).

In 278 B.C. Berosus, a pagan Chaldean historian, wrote in his, *Babylonian History*, that in his day people continued to go to Mount Ararat (the place where the Bible says Noah's ark rested) in order to gather pieces of the ruined ark for their supposed magical properties.[64]

So, the world was underwater. All left behind had died. The Nephilim, the hybrids, those part angel, part human creatures, perished, too. Isaiah 26:13-14 mentions there will be no resurrection for the Nephilim who are called Rephaim after the flood. It says, *"O LORD our God, other lords beside thee have had dominion over us: but by thee only will we make mention of thy name. They are dead;* (indicating they were once alive) *they shall not live; they are deceased* (that word is *rapha/raphah* and means ghosts of the dead, it also means giants) ***they shall not rise:*** *therefore hast thou visited and destroyed them, and made all their memory to perish."*

The dead Nephilim and Rephaim would be left to wander as disembodied spirits or demons looking to possess others like the Gadarene in Luke 8:26-33.

Satan had come close to destroying the seed. But there remained a few souls that could still thwart his plan. Preventing God's judicial decree from coming to pass still required the corruption of that seed. That meant Satan would have to try again.

Another Try

Satan had been busy. By the time the Israelites reached the promised land of Canaan, the giants were entrenched. No longer called the Nephilim or "fallen ones" they were now referred to as Rephaim or "the weakened ones." Apparently, they were not as strong or powerful as the Nephilim, but these post-flood giants were still fierce and warlike. And Satan must have been confident they were up to the task of thwarting the Hebrews.

It was hardly a surprise that the land was so full of giants. God had, once again, given away His game plan. When He made a covenant with Abraham it signaled that the Seed was to come from this bloodline. Now, Satan could toy with the rest of mankind, leisurely picking them off one-by-one. But the Hebrews, they had to be *crushed*.

Embedded in Genesis 6:2-4 was the warning that this would happen. *"the sons of God saw the daughters of men that they were fair; and they took them wives of all which they chose . . . There were giants in the earth in those days; **and also after that**, when the sons of God came in unto the daughters of men, and they bear children* *to them, the same became mighty men which were of old, men of renown."*

So, twice we are told that the sons of God cohabitated with women. And the phrase, *"in those days and also after that,"* indicates this occurred during two different time periods. It also has another meaning. When God says something twice in Scripture it means the thing is established and will not change. In other words, it was irreversible and could not be undone. Thus, what these angels did, could not be undone. And there would be no redemption for them or their partially human offspring.

So, how did this happen the second time?

Here are the three theories:
1. Ham's wife carried Nephilim DNA
2. human DNA was corrupted by fallen angles through occult practices and forbidden knowledge
3. fallen angels again cohabitated with women to produce offspring

I favor number three because it aligns with Scripture. In Genesis 6:2-4 both incursions are connected to angels having sex with women. In addition, the ancient rabbis (referenced in Niddah 61a) claimed Og, the giant and king of Bashan during Moses and Joshua's day, was the grandson of Shamhazai, the same fallen angel mentioned in the *Book of Enoch*, though in that book his name is spelled Semyaza. So, apparently the angels once again cohabitate with women after the flood.

But let's look at the theory that Ham's wife carried Nephilim DNA thus corrupting Ham's children and producing giants. It's true that most of the hybrid giants in the Middle East came from the line of Ham. But there were giants elsewhere, those coming from the line of Japheth. They included the Celtic, Norse, French, Gomarian, and Russian (Magog) giants. To this day, every November there is a parade in London, a parade that has been taking place for hundreds of years, and is headed by the city's Lord Mayor who walks alongside two huge replicas of their patron guardians—the giants Gog and Magog.[65] London, itself, is named after Lugus, an Irish god often portrayed as a giant.[66]

Then regarding the corruption of human DNA through occult practices or forbidden knowledge, this is a possibility because right now scientists can alter DNA by a simple kit called CRISPR-Cas9.

But if our scientists have this knowledge, you can be sure the fallen angels did, too. We need to understand that the ancients had incredible knowledge, much of it given them by fallen angels. The historian, Berosus, claimed that before the flood there was a "Town of Books" in Babylon and said that Noah, *"is made to bury his books at Sippara before the Deluge, and to disentomb them after the descent from the Ark."* Evidence also indicates there were universities, observatories and libraries in Larsa, Erech, Ur, and Cutha,[67] all ancient cities in Sumer (Babylon-Iraq).

It's possible that the corruption of human DNA after the flood was the result of both fallen angels cohabitating with women *and* the use of occult knowledge. But whichever way it occurred, it more than likely started at the Tower of Babel. Basically, the tower was a stargate or portal, a place to study the planetary bodies and practice astrology as well as interact with another dimension. The very word "Babel" means "gate of the gods" or "gate of the illumined ones." And the word "Nimrod" means, "let us revolt." And that's what they were doing.

We can assume that Nimrod had access to the books Berosus claimed Noah buried. And they must have contained some of the knowledge given to man by the angels, both holy and fallen. The *Book of Enoch* itself was full of such information. But obviously this was not enough for Nimrod. He desired to create a portal where once again fallen angels could return and intermingle with humans as well as teach occultic arts like they did in the past.

Nimrod knew how wicked his actions were because he feared God might react by bringing another flood, even though God had promised He'd never flood the earth again and even provided a symbol of that promise—the rainbow.

Nevertheless, Nimrod's tower was built of brick and covered with bitumen or slime just like the ark in order to waterproof it. Doing this was not only an act of rebellion but arrogance because it was telling God that in case you flood us again, we will be able to withstand it in our high, waterproof tower.

Though Nimrod knew how offensive his actions were, his desire to be god-like was stronger than his fear of the Lord. And this behavior made him Satan's ally, someone willing to create a one world government. This was Satan's second attempt at creating such a government. In the Garden of Eden, his first attempt had been successful, enabling him to become *"god of this world."* But in many ways mankind had proven unruly. They would be easier to control if they were all subject to one government. And with his help, Nimrod could be just the one to pull it off.

But God would not have it.

Genesis 11:5-8 says, *"And the LORD came down to see the city and the tower, which the children of men builded. And the LORD said, Behold the people is one, and they have all one language; and this they begin to do: and now nothing will be restrained from them which they have imagined to do. Go to, let us go down, and there confound their language, that they may not understand one another's speech. So the LORD scattered them abroad from thence upon the face of all the earth: and they left off to build the city."*

What a merciful solution by a merciful God! Instead of dispensing a harsh punishment for this new rebellious act, God scatters the people by changing their language. Along with the flood, the story of the Tower of Babel is embedded in the history of most cultures as illustrated by an ancient Babylonian tablet which says: *"The building of this illustrious tower offended the gods. In a night they threw down what they had built. They scattered them abroad, and made strange their speech."*[68]

As previously stated, many giants came from the line of Ham, including Nimrod who was Ham's grandson. Genesis 10:9 says Nimrod was, *"a mighty hunter before the Lord."* This has a negative meaning. It indicates Nimrod pitted himself against God. He was a rebel. And that word "mighty" is *gibbor* and can refer to someone strong and powerful, but it can also mean, "tyrant, giant, arrogant." It's the same word used when describing the Nephilim in Genesis 6.

Nimrod, the "mighty hunter," is often depicted as a giant holding a lion—the size of a house cat—under one arm, while holding a snake in the other hand. It's the same way Gilgamesh, a king and hero in ancient Sumerian mythology, who was believed to be part human and part divine and worshiped as god, is depicted. There is even a Hungarian legend that describes Nimrod as a giant as well as a "most wicked son from the line of Noah."[69]

Nimrod was the first king mentioned in the Bible. As his legend grew, he and his family began to be worshipped as gods by their descendants. Later, they became the basis of the "gods" of Rome, Greece and Egypt. Cush, Nimrod's father, became known as Mercury, "an Egyptian synonym for the 'son of Ham'."[70] Nimrod was also known as Gilgamesh, Kronos, Osiris, Horus, Tammuz, Bacchus, Marduk, Baal, Orion, Apollo, and Dionysus.[71]

Ancestor worship became common worldwide. As other Rephaim died, their descendants began worshiping and venerate them as gods, too. They not only became the "gods" of the pantheon in Greece but became gods under various names throughout the ancient world. One example: many of the gods in Hindu myths are depicted as giants as well as part animal part human.[72]

But what's interesting is that the character traits of these "gods" were like the character traits of the Nephilim/Rephaim. They were licentious, bullies, tyrants, selfish, violent and produced children with women—the so-called "demigods."

At this point, a brief summary of the Nimrod legend is necessary because it will greatly factor into what happens later. It is said he married Semiramis, a prostitute who he claimed was a goddess. She had an illicit affair and when Nimrod found out, she killed her husband and claimed her illegitimate child was the savior promised in Genesis, and that Nimrod was both the father and child. The child was named Tammuz, the same Tammuz mentioned in Ezekiel 8:14-15, *"Then he (God) brought me to the door of the gate of the LORD's house which was toward the north; and, behold there sat women weeping for **Tammuz**. Then said he unto me. Hast thou seen this, O son of man? turn thee yet again, and thou shalt see greater abominations than these."*

Later, Nimrod's legend was converted into Egyptian lore where Nimrod became the sun god, Ra, as well as Osiris, while Semiramis became Isis (and Astarte, Diana, Ashtoreth in other cultures), and her son, who she claimed was also Nimrod, became both Osiris and Horus. It's from this that we get the "Eye of Ra" or "Eye of Horus."[73]

But in the Egyptian version, the version that will have far reaching consequences, Osiris/Nimrod is killed by his evil brother, Seth, and cut into fourteen pieces which are thrown into the Nile. After searching, Isis/Semiramis finally finds thirteen of them. The missing piece? His genitals, which is replaced by an obelisk and magically impregnates her with Horus/Nimrod.

This culture was hardly ignorant of the true God and man's fall. A sculpture, perhaps the oldest intact depiction of Adam and Eve in a garden with a serpent and tree, was found in the Temple of Osiris at Phylae.[74] This makes the veneration of Osiris/Nimrod more egregious. It's obvious that many people preferred to participate in forbidden occultic arts and to worship demigods rather than the True God. And they either participated in forbidden occult rituals or outright cohabitated with the fallen angels to produce the Rephaim.

As previously stated, by the time the Israelites arrived, there were plenty of giants living in the Promised Land. God specifically ordered Joshua and his army to annihilate them. These giants were not those who suffered from a condition known as gigantism, and which is caused by over-production of growth hormones or a tumor on the pituitary gland or a genetic mutation. People with gigantism usually experience multiple health issues, are generally weak because of the stress on their skeletal system, and normally have a short life span. Very different from the giants of the Bible who were strong and war-like.

1 Samuel 17:5-7 talks about Goliath's armor weighing 5000 shekels of brass. According to the internet that's 125 pounds. Numbers 13 talks about how the twelve spies, after going into the Promised Land, bring back an evil report about the giants, the sons of Anak, and how they felt like grasshoppers in their sight. They must have been large, indeed!

Deuteronomy 3:11 talks about Og, King of Bashan, a giant whose bed was nine cubits. A cubit is 18 to 22 inches which means Og's bed was between 13 to 16 feet long. This is the same Og the ancient rabbis claimed was the grandson of the fallen angel, Shamhazai.

The giants are called many names in the Bible: Emim, Zamzummim, Rephaim, Anakim, etcetera. And according to the Bible, these giants had similar traits. They were huge, strong, tyrants, bullies and many were cannibals. Numbers 13:32 says, *"The land, through which we* (the Israelite spies) *have gone to search it, is a land that **eateth up the inhabitants** thereof."*

The giants also had unique physical characteristics such as double rows of teeth, six fingers on each hand and six toes on each foot. It's interesting to note that when Michael Angelo painted the Cumaean Sibyl (the oldest of the Sibyls and oracle of the underworld) on the Sistine Chapel, he painted her with six fingers, though one was cut off at the knuckle.[75]

2 Samuel and 1 Chronicles talk about the Valley of Rephaim or Valley of Giants. And Bashan, where Og lived and which is the location of Mt. Herman, the very mountain where the 200 angels descended, was called the Land of the Giants. Jericho was known as the "city of the giants."[76] And Canaan and Transjordan were both known as the Land of the Rephaim.[77] Also, there once was a cave-city between Jerusalem and Gaza called Beit Jibrim or House of the Gibborim.[78] And as we've seen, gibborim is just another word for giant. There are many more such

references, but the above is enough to show that the Promised Land was populated by giants. Since the Seed would come from the Jews, Satan made sure the greatest concentration of giants was in the land promised them.

According to the *Book of Jubilees*, there were giants also in Sodom and Gomorra. Jude 6 talks about the angels who left their first estate, while verse 7 goes on to talk about Sodom and Gomorrah. *"Even as Sodom and Gomorrah, and the cities about them in like manner, giving themselves over to fornication, and going after **strange flesh**, are set forth for an example, suffering the vengeance of eternal fire."*

That word, "strange" means, "other, different, altered," and "flesh" indicates flesh or the body. So, when Jude talks about "strange flesh" it indicates different or altered flesh. He's not talking about sodomy or the sexual interaction between men, which was also prevalent. Rather, Jude 6-7 links together the occurrence of the Nephilim/Rephaim in both Noah's day and Lot's day and their sexual encounters with women.

Among the Dead Sea Scrolls is a manuscript called, *Testaments of the 12 Patriarchs*. These are believed to be the writings of the Patriarchs preserved by the Essenes. In the *Testament of Naphtali*, Naphtali writes, *"Do not become like Sodom, who changed the order of their nature, in the **same manner** as the Watchers* (angels) *changed the order of their nature. They are the cause of the Flood and the desolation of the earth."*[79]

Once Jesus, the Seed, came was that the end of the giants?

No.

Satan's fate was now sealed. The judicial decree could not be nullified. But since the Seed had yet to claim His rightful earthly throne, it meant there was still time for Satan to vent his hatred for God by destroying the things He loved. Taking every human to hell with him and trying to steal those he could from the family of God, would now be his primary mission. The Cosmic War was far from over.

So, giants continued on the earth and were, in fact, a world-wide phenomenon. Stephen Quayle, in his book, *Genesis 6 Giants,* covers this in detail. In it, he relates the legends of giants around the world as well as describing their physical evidence in various places. I highly recommend it for those who would like to know more. His research uncovered giants in North and South America, Europe, Asia, Africa,

Australia and, of course, the Middle East. They were mound builders and their mounds are located everywhere. The Serpent Mound near Louden, OH, Monks Mound in Illinois, and many many others show them to be prolific builders.

And Chaco Canyon in Colorado, Casas Grandes, Polacca Washington, Ash Creek, Rattlesnake Ruin and others provide proof of their cannibalism.[80] In addition, many giants throughout the world had the familiar six fingers and toes and double rows of teeth. They also left behind a trail of violence and bloodshed.

Ok, but what about archeological evidence of Giants?

Most were found hundreds of years ago. But many have disintegrated due to being poorly maintained, leaving more written records than physical ones. Nevertheless, there are some. In fact, archeology and history books written in the 1800s are full of these discoveries.

Some physical finds include:

26-foot giant found in Bohemia in 758, whose leg bone is still supposedly stored in a castle.[81]

A 25-foot giant called "Theutobochus Rex" was found in France in 1613.[82]

30-foot giants were found in 1548 and 1550 in Sicily.[83]

8 to 10-foot giants found in the California Humbolt Lakebed.[84]

12-foot giant with double rows of teeth was found, 1833, in Lompock Rancho, California.[85]

9-foot giants found in Crittenden, Arizona, 1891, during the digging of a foundation.[86]

9-foot giants found 1947 in Death Valley by amateur archeologists who said their graves also contained dinosaur and tiger bones.[87]

In the 1950s, a 15-foot giant was found during road construction in southeast Turkey. Also found were tombs containing giants.

There are others, but again I suggest you read *Genesis 6 Giants* or *True Legends* for those details.

Would it surprise you to learn that early explorers to America saw living giants? It did me. Magellan, Sir Francis Drake, Commodore Byron, and Anthony

Knyvet all claimed to have seen them. Pigafetta, a crewmember on Magellan's fleet, describes what he saw: *"This man was so tall that our heads scarcely came up to his waist, and his voice was like that of a bull."*[88]

Then in the 20th and 21st centuries, things changed. Stories of giants began to disappear, and their bones and artifacts began to be systematically hidden.

Noted Native American author and retired law professor, Vine Deloria, blames the Smithsonian and said, *"the Smithsonian Institution created a one-way portal through which uncounted bones have been spirited. This door and the contents of its vault are virtually sealed off to any but government officials."*[89]

If that's true, then the question is, "why?"

The Smithsonian is a marvelous place, a wonder-land of exhibits that would take weeks to do justice. I really love the place. Established in 1847, it's now a behemoth, consisting of research centers, libraries and museums.

But early in its inception, it went astray. Beginning about 1867, John W. Powell, acting for the institute, lead the exploration of the Colorado canyons during which time artifacts were found that did not jive with his Theory of Evolution. Among them were bones of giants. He relegated these finds to "anomalies" and therefore not relevant to his research. As more and more of these "anomalies" were discovered they continued to be ignored and even excluded from his reports as well as systematically suppressed.[90] A precedent was set. And in 1907, it became known as the "Powell Doctrine."

This precedent was continued, in 1910, by his successor, Ales Hrdlicka. An advocate of eugenics and evolution, Hrdlicka had no interest in rocking the then established position of evolution held by the Smithsonian higher ups and backers. Thus, the coverup continued.[91]

But the existence of these bones, if known, would do more than destroy the Theory of Evolution. It would validate the Bible, the creation story and the existence of God. And Satan couldn't allow that, so he used men, who had their own agendas, to cover it up and keep it covered.

For the most part, God has decimated the giants. But that wouldn't prove a hardship for Satan. He didn't need them anymore or at least not for a while. What he had lost with the giants, he had gained through Darwin. More and more people believed they had crawled out of the primordial soup. Society was losing its Scriptural mooring. And that would make the success of the next phase easier to achieve.

America: One Nation Two Foundations

Satan had done a masterful job in the Old Word. His minions had many powerful and influential people in their pockets. And already much of the so-called New World, which was hardly new, for he had been preparing it for decades, was under his thumb. The land was ready. Years of human bloodletting had ripened it, made it fertile for his next step. The region's southern soil was soaked from sacrifices made by the Aztec's in his, Quetzalcoatl's, honor as well as in some of his other names. And the northern regions were also drenched through tribal wars. And all had been pleasing offerings. But now he had to act. He needed to get his plan in place before the Most High implemented His. It would be a race, but he was confident it would be his to win.

However, Satan's initial attempts didn't turn out as expected. The first two colonies founded in America were unsuccessful. The Roanoke Colony, organized and financed by Sir Walter Raleigh, was founded in 1584 in North Carolina. It was also called the Lost Colony because by 1590 it was abandoned and its inhabitants never seen again.[92] The second colony, began 1607 in Popham Beach, Maine, dissolved a little over a year later in 1608.[93]

But then things began looking up. Around the time the Popham Colony was being established, three ships, the *Susan Constant, Discovery* and *Godspeed*, were anchoring off the shores of what would become known as Jamestown.[94] The colony was established by the Virginia Company of London, a company founded by members of secret, occult societies whose membership included Sir Francis Bacon. Its charter was like that of the other two colonies: secure riches and trade for the crown of England. This colony, and indeed the American continent, was considered by Sir Francis Bacon to be the *New Atlantis* after Plato's Atlantis which was not only a civilization of advanced technology and war-like demigods, but was also considered the "Golden Age of Osiris (Nimrod)." All this would factor into American Freemason ideology.[95]

The primary purpose of all three colonies was to find a Northwest Passage to Asia and the pursuit of wealth via trade, as well as by extracting rich minerals, including gold, from America and filling England's coffers. It was also intended "to make America the head of the *New Atlantis*." In other words, the springboard for the New World Order.[96]

Both Sir Walter Raleigh (financier of the Roanoke Colony, politician, and landed gentleman) and Sir Francis Bacon (attorney general and Lord Chancellor of England) played major roles in the British colonization of North America. According to Manly P. Hall, a Freemason and important figure in the metaphysical movement of the 1920s, Raleigh and Bacon were members of the same secret society, School of Night, which embraced Rosicrucian ideology. In fact, the Rosicrucian organization, AMORC, states Bacon led their movement in England and throughout Europe.[97]

The Rosicrucian movement became popular in Europe during the early 1600s. Members believed they could "reform humanity" through secret knowledge, much of it passed down from ancient Egypt. Its manifesto declared that their "secret brotherhood" would change the intellectual environment of Europe. It went on to birth other "secret societies" including the Freemasons.

It was while acting as its head that Bacon conceived his secret occult plan for America. Almost 170 years later, The Rosicrucian Order merged with the Bavarian Illuminati, founded in 1776 by Adam Weishaupt, but was banned ten years later by the government and forced to go underground. And that's where it remains, with many branches worldwide busily working for the creation of the *New Atlantis.*[98]

While the Virginia Company was busy trying to create this *New Atlantis*, along comes another group. And when the *Mayflower* dropped anchor is 1620, a very different colony was established, that of Plymouth in Massachusetts. The bulk of the settlers were Puritans, seeking to escape religious persecution, though among the landing party were some secular tradesmen, soldiers and adventurers. These Puritans came in search of a better life, but more importantly they desired a place to freely worship God and to advance the gospel. Rather than a *New Atlantis*, their desire was to establish a *New Jerusalem.*[99]

John Winthrop, who became the first governor of the Massachusetts Bay Colony, expressed this in his sermon as he and the Puritans crossed the Atlantic.

> *"The eyes of the world will be upon us. We are as a city upon a hill, raised up. You may think we're in the howling wilderness. You may think we're out beyond the farthest beyond. But in fact, God's providence is such that as the latter days begin to unfold, this may indeed be the city, the new Jerusalem that's unfolding before not only our eyes but the eyes of the world."*[100]

These Puritans saw themselves as a "kingdom of believers." Their mission: to create a holy commonwealth. The Mayflower Compact was drafted onboard ship and signed by forty-one out of the hundred and one passengers (mostly Puritans) and was the "seed of American democracy."[101]

The Mayflower Compact reads:

"IN THE NAME OF GOD, AMEN. We, whose names are underwritten, the Loyal Subjects of our dread sovereign Lord King James, by the Grace of God, of Great Britain, France, and Ireland, King, Defender of the Faith, & Having undertaken for the Glory of God and Advancement of the Christian Faith, and the Honour of our King and Country, a Voyage to plant the first Colony in the northern Parts of Virginia; Do by these Presents, solemnly and mutually, in the Presence of God and one another, covenant and combine ourselves together into a civil Body Politick, for our better Ordering and Preservation, and Furtherance of the Ends aforesaid: And by Virtue hereof do enact, constitute, and frame, such just and equal Laws, Ordinances, Acts, Constitutions, and Officers, from time to time, as shall be thought most meet and convenient for the general Good of the Colony, unto which we promise all due Submission and Obedience.

"IN WITNESS whereof we have hereunto subscribed our names at Cape-Cod the eleventh of November, in the Reign of our Sovereign Lord King James, of England, France, and Ireland, the eighteenth, and of Scotland the fifty-fourth, Anno Domini, 1620. "

Then it's followed by forty-one signatures.[102]

From the beginning, America was founded on two very different belief systems. One would lead to freedom of religion, with Christianity becoming the bulwark, the other to a secret Luciferian network. And it would be only a matter of time before the plan of God for America and the plan of Satan for America would collide.

The Christian influence:

The Christian influence has spread far and wide. America is known for sending missionaries to evangelize the globe as well as help impoverished people groups. Out of Judeo-Christian laws and values, America's judicial system was born. America has also raised up great men and women of God like Cotton Mather, Jonathan Edwards, Charles F. Parham, William J. Seymour, Kathryn Kuhlman. William Branham, Jack Coe and A.A. Allen. It saw the Great Awakening in the 1730s-40s as well as Azusa Street in 1906 and the copious tent revivals throughout the 20th Century. Its true influence will only be fully known in the hereafter.

The Luciferian network:

But what came out of the first three colonies is equally far reaching. These colonies were based on greed, conquest, forbidden knowledge, and a hidden agenda. From the Rosicrucians came the Freemasons, a secret society that today impacts our nation in ways we can't even imagine.

What is Freemasonry?

American Masonry can be traced to the time of Sir Francis Bacon's England of 1561-1626. Bacon is considered its first Grand Master. Associated with Bacon was Dr. John Dee, Queen Elizabeth I's astrologer who sought secret knowledge through contact with demons.[103] It was Dee who introduced England's royalty to the occult.

Manly P. Hall, (1901-1990) who was a 33rd Degree Freemason, author, astrologer and mystic, describes Masonry as, *"a fraternity within a fraternity—an outer organization concealing an inner brotherhood of the elect . . . it is necessary to establish the existence of these two separate yet interdependent orders, the one visible and the other invisible. The visible society is a splendid camaraderie of 'free and accepted' men enjoined to devote themselves to ethical, educational, fraternal, patriotic, and humanitarian concerns. The invisible society is a secret and most august fraternity whose members are dedicated to the service of a mysterious arcanum arcanorum (a secret or mystery). In each generation, only a few are accepted into the inner sanctuary of the work.*"[104]

Masonry is replete with secret rites which includes kneeling before a trapezoid-shaped altar, which represents Nimrod's unfinished work at Babel. This same type of altar can be seen in the UN Meditation Room. The supplicant then asks the Worshipful Master of the Lodge for light, which Albert Pike, the leading Masonic philosopher in the 1800s, identified as Lucifer. The supplicant swears an oath that he will never reveal what he is about to learn. Should he violate this oath, he acknowledges that his throat will be cut, and his tongue torn out. Reaching the second level of Masonry he acknowledges if he violates his oath his breast will be torn open and his heart plucked out. The third-degree initiate acknowledges that an oath violation would be followed by his body cut in half and his bowels removed and burned.

According to Albert Pike, these three degrees were called The Blue Degrees. Regarding them, he said they are, *"but the outer court or portico of the Temple. Part of the symbols are displayed there to the Initiate, but he is intentionally misled by false interpretations. It is not intended that he shall understand them; but it is intended that he shall imagine he understands them. Their true explication is reserved for the Adepts, the Princes of Masonry."*[105] It's interesting to note that the initiation into the Blue Lodge is the same initiation one undergoes when initiated into a witch's coven.[106]

Pike also said, *"Masonry . . . conceals its secrets from all except the Adepts and Sages, or the Elect, and uses false explanations and misinterpretations of its symbols to mislead those who deserve only to be misled; to conceal the Truth, which it calls Light, from them, and to draw them away from it."*[107]

Manly P. Hall, the icon of Freemasonry, confirms this. *"The rise of the Christian Church broke up the intellectual pattern of the classical pagan world. By persecution . . . it drove the secret societies into greater secrecy: the pagan intellectuals then reclothed their original ideas in a garment of Christian phraseology, but bestowed the keys of the symbolism only upon those duly initiated and bound to secrecy by their vows."*[108]

So, we see that Masonry is entwined with lies and deception. And why not? Satan, their master, is a liar. In fact, Jesus, in John 8:44, called him the father of lies. In Masonry, the higher ups deceive their members as well as deceive the world-at-large by using Christian phraseology to cover-up their true nature and purpose. But both nature and purpose are clearly reflected by Masonry's own Supreme Council which apply the following descriptions to members of various degrees. The Council calls, "the 1st degree through the 11th of their membership, 'slaves of Lucifer,' and the 12th through 22nd, 'pontiffs of Lucifer.' As for those who become a 33rd degree Mason, they refer to themselves as being 'a sovereign of Lucifer'."[109]

While members of the lower ranks are kept in darkness, by the time an initiate reaches the highest level, if he reaches it, it all becomes clear. Manly P. Hall says it this way, "*When the Mason . . . has learned the mystery of his Craft. The seething energies of **Lucifer** are in his hands.*" Thus, when Masons bow before The Worshipful Master and recite their vows during their various initiations, they are making those vows to Satan.

Albert Pike was also Sovereign Grand Commander of the Scottish Rite, a branch of Freemasonry which only grants entrance to a Master Mason, one who has completed the three degrees of Blue Lodge Masonry. He was a man who understood the deep inner workings of Freemasonry and openly stated, *"The true and pure philosophic religion is the belief in Lucifer."*[110] High ranking Masons understand that when they pray or refer to the Lord or God, they are referring to Satan. In addition, many of them belong to the Illuminati and are Satanists who claim they possess the Light of Lucifer. Also, many in the Illuminati also claim they are descendants of the Nephilim.

Before we go further, it is important to note that Freemasons have a ceremony they enact called the "raising ceremony" which involves someone called Hiram Abiff, the supposed architect of Solomon's temple. This enactment occurs during special occasions and involves the portrayal of Abiff's death, burial and future resurrection. In truth, it's the reenactment of the legend of Isis and Osiris (Nimrod) and symbolizes Masonry's belief that Nimrod will rise again.

Recall from the last chapter that Osiris is the Egyptian personification of Nimrod, the rebel who built the Tower of Babel. And to recap, in the Egyptian version Osiris (Nimrod) is killed by his evil brother, Seth, and cut into fourteen pieces which are thrown into the Nile. After searching for them, Isis, who was really Nimrod's wife, Semiramis, finally finds thirteen of them. The missing piece is his genitals, which is replaced by an obelisk and magically impregnates her with Horus who is also Nimrod.

How has this affected America?

Manly P. Hall said, *"Men bound by a secret oath to labor in the cause of world democracy decided that in the **American colonies** they would plant the roots of a new way of life. Brotherhoods were established to meet secretly, and they quietly and industriously conditioned America to its destiny for leadership in a free world."*[111]

Beginning with Sir Walter Raleigh and Sir Francis Bacon, secret societies have been quietly working to bring about, in America and elsewhere, their *New Atlantis*, their idea of Utopia, a perfect society without the God of the Bible. And from that time to this, our history is marred with their handiwork.

More than half of the signers of the Declaration of Independence were Masons. And many U.S. Presidents, both Democrat and Republican, were Masons. But Freemasonry includes other diverse movers-and-shakers. From bankers to newspaper and media moguls to corporate CEOs to politicians and heads of state, their ranks continue to burgeon.

Washington D.C. itself is full of Freemasonry symbolism. The actual city was designed by a Masonic architect and is laid out in an incomplete pentagram. Many federal buildings have Masonic cornerstones, and all "bear a Masonic plaque."[112] The Washington Monument symbolizes the erect phallus of Nimrod. The Capitol dome is the impregnated womb of Isis, symbolizing the magical rebirth and resurrection of Nimrod from the underworld. Amazingly, this same set up is repeated at the Vatican in Rome, which also has strong ties to Freemasonry. It includes an obelisk and dome, again Freemasonry symbols of Nimrod and Isis. The obelisk also represents the sun god Ra, which, as previously stated in the last chapter, is none other than Nimrod.

But that's not the end of it. On the back of the dollar is the Great Seal of the United States. It features the "All-Seeing Eye" or "Eye of Horus or Ra (Nimrod)." It, too, appears in the UN Meditation Room. Also, on the back of the dollar is an unfinished pyramid, symbolizing Nimrod's unfinished work which Freemasons believe will be completed after Nimrod is resurrected. It is the goal of Freemasonry and the Illuminati to prepare the way for Nimrod's resurrection so he can complete the work he began.

Also, on the back of the dollar are the words, *"novus ordo seclorum"* meaning "a new order for the centuries."[113] It's referring to and advertising the coming of the New World Order.

Here's how Manly Hall explained some of the above. *"Not only were many of the founders of the United States Government Masons, but they received aid from a secret and august body existing in Europe, which helped them to establish this country for a peculiar and particular purpose known only to the initiated few. The Great Seal is the signature of this exalted body—unseen and for the most part unknown—and the unfinished pyramid upon its reverse side is a trestle board setting forth symbolically the task to the accomplishment of which the United States Government was **dedicated from the day of its inception.**"*[114]

The raising ceremony, symbolizing the resurrection of Nimrod, is conducted each time a Freemason reaches the level of Master. But what's disturbing is that this same ceremony is also conducted after the election of every U.S. President! What does it represent? The same thing it represented when performed in the Egyptian temple of Amun-Ra when priests attempted to install the spirit of Osiris (Nimrod) into their new pharaoh. What the Freemasons are doing after each election is using occult practices to infuse the new president with this spirit until Nimrod himself resurrects and fulfills the Great Seal prophecy.[115]

Manly P. Hall in his, *The Secret Teaching of All Ages,* wrote, "*The Dying God* (Osiris/Nimrod) *shall rise again! The secret room in the House of the Hidden Places shall be rediscovered. The Pyramid again shall stand as the ideal emblem of . . . resurrection, and regeneration.*"[116] The *Ancient Egyptian Pyramid Texts* also claims Osiris/Nimrod will rise again.[117]

Revelation 9:11 talks about a king over the bottomless pit named Apollyon, which is just another name for Nimrod. Revelation calls this king an "angel." He is king over creatures that, during the seven-year Tribulation, are allowed to ascend from the pit and harass the inhabitants of earth for a short time. Revelation 9:7-10 describes them: they have faces of men, hair like women, lion's teeth, scorpion tails and wings. They appear to be hybrids: part man, part animal, part insect, part fallen angel.

Though I believe Nimrod was a hybrid himself, I'm not sure the Bible would call him an "angel." Therefore, I prefer to link Nimrod to the antichrist. I believe Nimrod is a type of antichrist and symbolic of what the antichrist will be: a tyrant, and rebel against God. He will be someone who desires to create a One World Government and One World

Religion featuring, first, Mystery Babylon, the harlot and mother of all false religions, then himself enthroned as god. To accomplish this, he must be empowered by Satan. Many in the occult today are praying to Satan for Nimrod's arrival. In the meantime, they are working to build a One World Government or New World Order in preparation for Nimrod's second coming. And for a time, during the seven-year Tribulation, it will look like he is prevailing over God himself.

What can we take away from all this?

Freemasonry is a secret and deceptive organization, deceiving even its own members as well as the world, and concealing the fact that their allegiance is to Satan. Their goal is a One World Government, headed by their god, Nimrod (Osiris) which they believe will resurrect in bodily form to head this government and create a *New Atlantis*. Meanwhile, the Luciferian elite are working hard to facilitate this.

The Bible tells us that a house divided cannot stand. That's what we are seeing now—America divided as both foundations, one founded on Godly principles, the other on forbidden secret knowledge, vie for dominance.

The New Atlantis

Has the *New Atlantis* gained inroads in America? The one attempted by Nimrod then envisioned by Sir Walter Raleigh and Sir Francis Bacon? The one carried on by the Freemasons and Illuminati as the very model of the antichrist's future end-times empire?

Yes, much to Satan's delight.

Nimrod's secret occult knowledge has been passed down through generations via the numerous secret societies dedicated to creating this *New Atlantis* or, in the modern vernacular, the New World Order. This secret knowledge has spread through "Egypt, Rome, China, South America" and finally North America, and carries with it the concept of "god-kings" who ruled their empire through three major systems: spiritual, political, and economic.[118] The final "god-king," of course, is supposed to be Nimrod/Osiris who, the secret societies believe, will resurrect at the proper time. That explains why occult reproduction is at the very center of the mystery religions.

Tom Horn, in his book, *Apollyon Rising*, says, *"According to Virgil and the Cumaean Sibyl, whose prophecy formed the **novus ordo seclorum** of the Great Seal of the United States, the New World Order begins during a time of chaos when the earth and oceans are tottering—a time like today. This is when the 'son' of promise arrives on earth—Apollo incarnate—a pagan savior born of 'a new breed of men sent down from heaven when 'heroes' and 'gods' are blended together."* [119] Keep in mind that Apollo is just another name for Nimrod and that the motto of the New World Order is "Order out of Chaos."

The influence of these secret societies can be seen everywhere. The European Parliament building is called the "Tower of Eurobabel." Its poster even features Nimrod's tower. In addition, the statue of the goddess, Europa, riding a bull, sits outside the EU headquarters in Brussels.[120] If that doesn't conjure up an image of the whore of Babylon sitting on a beast, I don't know what does.

The now deceased UNs General Assembly's first president, Paul-Henri Spaak, made this outrageous statement: *"We don't want another committee, we have too many already. What we want is a man of sufficient stature to hold the allegiance of all the people and to lift us up out of the economic crisis into which we are sinking.*

*Send us such a man, whether he be God or **devil**, we will receive him."*[121]

What kind of society would welcome help from a devil or the demonic realm? The kind that has lost its spiritual mooring and has become morally bankrupt!

The concept of a *New Atlantis* or New World Order is so widespread and appears so desirable that even notable people have boarded its train. Winston Churchill, Franklin Roosevelt, Harry Truman, Cecil Rhodes, John D. Rockefeller, J.P. Morgan, Bush Sr., and many others all have espoused a One World Government.[122] In 2011, even Pope Benedict XVI called for the creation of a New World Order.[123]

Both socialism and communism were birthed out of this desire. Rockefeller made loans to the Bolsheviks during their revolution, as did the Morgan banks. In addition, J.P. Morgan's companies helped finance the American Communist Party.[124]

In former Georgetown professor, Carroll Quigley's book, *Tragedy and Hope: A History of the World in Our Times,* he makes this startling statement, *"the powers of financial capitalism had another far-reaching aim, nothing less than to create a world system of financial control in private hands able to dominate the political system of each country and the economy of the world as a whole."*[125]

Newspaper journalist, Jim Marrs, in his book, *Our Occulted History* says that the global financial power, *"employs a variety of means to enrich itself, including 'fraud, deception, assassination, and war,' in order to 'usurp the money and credit creating power of the various states it has sought to dominate.'"*[126]

Magazine editor, David Rothkopf, who wrote about the global elite, claims that between six to seven thousand wealthy globalists "run the world's governments, largest corporations, powerhouses of international finance, media, and religions."[127]

Knowing that messaging is everything and can change mindsets and form new ones, the global elites have carefully gained control of our media, which is now in the hands of only six major corporations. And even fewer groups control our educational systems. The fruits of this are evident in the fact that today 30% of young Americans believe socialism and communism are desirable.[128]

The global elites make up the "shadow government" which is connected to various secret societies such as the Freemasons, Bohemian Grove, Skull and Bones, and the Illuminati.

This certainly makes it easier to understand what's going on with Donald Trump. Yes, he can be crude or brash, and sometimes not very presidential, but that's not why he's so hated, especially by other politicians, the media and elites. He is hated because he is a nationalist, an America-First guy and not a globalist. And that's driving the elites crazy. He is thwarting their globalist agenda, the agenda of the Luciferian elites to create a One World Government by undoing Obama's regulations and draining the very swamp they have controlled for years. And they don't like it!

There are at least seven shadow organizations trying to bring about a One World Government and that also means a One World Religion.

The Rosicrucians, members of an ancient secret Egyptian society, were the forerunners of the Freemasons, which, according to *Regius*, a Masonic manuscript written in 1390, cites Nimrod as its, *"first and most excellent master."* Later, their 1756 manuscript, *Thistle*, claims Nimrod, *"created the Masons."*[129]

From out of the Masons came the Illuminati which took hold in Europe during 1776 when it began promoting the idea of a New World Order. Karl Marx, the father of Communism, came out of the

Illuminati. His *Communist Manifesto* was virtually a replica of *The Illuminati Manifesto*.

The rise of secular humanism, which ironically has been declared a "religion," is facilitating the march toward the *New Atlantis*. Their primary goal is to create a global society and to establish a social and economic order for the redistribution of wealth. It rejects the human need for salvation and believes Christian salvation to be "harmful." Their *Humanist Manifesto* also mirrors both Illuminati beliefs and socialist-communist principles. It claims that man must create his own religion, and seeks these seventeen objectives:

1. Rejection of traditional religion
2. Rejection of the concept of sin, salvation and the need for God
3. Promote idea that morals and ethics are situational
4. Push idea that a better world can be achieved through intelligence and reason
5. Encourage personal freedom without moral restrictions
6. Promote abortion, sexual exploration and divorce
7. Promote euthanasia and suicide
8. Promote democracy (mob rule) rather than a democratic republic

9. Promote concept of "separation of church and state"
10. Promote economic socialism
11. Promote government control over every area of life by using "anti-discrimination" as a tool
12. Destroy nationalism and promote concept of a "world community"
13. Promote the need for an international court
14. Promote environmentalism and population control
15. Provide aid and birth control to developing nations
16. Remove all barriers to scientific research
17. Promote international cooperation as absolutely essential[130]

The Illuminati is also promoting Islam while at the same time planning World War III—a war between Muslim and European nations. In the occult world, the crescent moon represents Nimrod's wife, Semiramis, and the star represents Nimrod. In many statues of him, one can see a crescent moon and star engraved near his waist.[131]

The end goal of the Illuminati is to rule mankind and the world by destroying all religion and governments.[132] To achieve this they plan to abolish private property and inheritances, patriotism, family life and marriage along with employing chaos, discord, confusion and the power of the bureaucracy.[133]

In his book, *The Committee of 300,* Dr. John Coleman said this of the Illuminati, *"In the Committee of 300, which has a 150-year history, we have some of the most brilliant intellects assembled to form a completely totalitarian, absolutely controlled 'new' society—only it isn't new, having drawn most of its ideas from the Clubs of Cultus Diabolicus. It strives toward a one world government."*[134]

Below are other relevant quotes:

"Behind the ostensible government sits enthroned an invisible government owing no allegiance and acknowledging no responsibility to the people" Theodore Roosevelt

"We shall have world government, whether or not we like it. The question is only whether world government will be achieved by consent or by conquest." James Warburg, son of Paul Warburg, "Father" of the Federal Reserve

"The drive of the Rockefellers and their allies is to create a one-world government combining super-capitalism and Communism under the same tent, all under their control

. . . Do I mean conspiracy? Yes, I do. I am convinced there is such a plot, international in scope, generations old in planning, and incredibly evil in intent." Larry MacDonald (1935-1985) former Democratic Representative from Georgia

"Out of these troubled times, our objective—a new world order—can emerge. Today, that new world order is struggling to be born, a world quite different from the one we have known." George H. W. Bush 41st President of the United States

During the years 1941-1971 the U.S. Supreme Court was controlled by Masons. And four Mason Supreme Court Justices were able to remove prayer and God from our public schools.[135]

The top ranks of the Freemans (33rd degree) are associated with the Illuminati. And the insignia of the Illuminati on back of our dollar—a pyramid and the all-seeing eye—should tell us the extent of their reach and power. It's not surprising then that six other organizations have come out of them: The Council on Foreign Relations, the UN, the Club of Rome, the Bilderberg, the Trilateral Commission, and the New Age Movement. I have already discussed these in my book, *12 Questions New Christians Frequently Ask,* but will recap some of the information here.

First: The Council on Foreign Relations, began in 1921, has worked hard to get the United States to back the idea of a One World Government. J.P. Morgan and Colonel House created this Council as a front for the Round Table Group, a group dedicated to one world governance. Admiral Chester Ward (Judge Advocate General of the Navy from 1956-1960) said this about them: *"The most powerful clique* (The Council on Foreign Relations) *in these elitist groups have one objective in common — they want to bring about the surrender of the sovereignty and the national independence of the United States."*[136]

Nearly all the top media corporations are Council members.[137] And out of the last nine U.S. presidents, six were also members.[138]

Second: The UN, which was founded in 1945. In 1980, it formulated a plan for the New World Order. In 1996 it detailed how to implement this plan in a 420-page document called, *Our Global Neighborhood.*

While no cross or other religious artifacts are displayed in or on UN grounds, a statue of Zeus is positioned near the entrance of the main lobby. The statue has been acknowledged as being that of Zeus since 1953 when it was gifted to the UN by the Greek government. Only recently has the UN claimed it's really a statue of Poseidon.

It's interesting to note that Zeus was referred to as "Satan" by Jesus (Revelation 2:12-13). In His letter, Jesus said Satan's seat was in Pergamos. The seat Jesus was referencing was the throne or altar of Zeus. In 1930, this throne was dismantled and taken to Berlin, Germany, where it currently resides in the Berlin Pergamon Museum.

In preparation for the New World Order, the UN has divided the world into ten designated zones.[139] To me, it's rather reminiscent of the ten toes in Daniel's prophecy (Daniel 2:41-42). The zones are as follows:

1) America, Canada, Mexico. (Perhaps this is why so many in the U.S. government are unwilling to secure our borders or do anything on immigration reform.)
2) South and Central America
3) Australia and New Zealand
4) Western Europe
5) Eastern Europe
6) Japan
7) South Asia
8) Central Asia
9) North Africa and Middle East
10) the rest of Africa

In the UN meditation room, there is a trapezoid-shaped altar like the trapezoid altar found in a Masonic lodge and represents Nimrod's unfinished work at Babel. Remember what Paul-Henri Spaak, the first UN president said. They would accept anyone who could help us out of our economic mess, *"whether he be God or **devil**."* His adherents will certainly get their wish when the demonically controlled antichrist takes over.

Third: The Bilderbergs, began 1954 in Holland. A secretive organization, it's behind the European Union. They had hoped to have everyone in the world implanted with a microchip by 2017. Obviously, they are behind schedule.

Phyllis Schlafly in her book, *A Choice Not An Echo*, describes a secret Bilderberg meeting in 1957 held in the King and Prince Hotel near St. Simon's Island, Georgia. *"Those who came were not the heads of states, but those who give orders to heads of states—in other words, the kingmakers."*[140] The strategy of the Bilderbergs is to bring "Order out of chaos." To achieve this, they must break down all our systems and create new ones. And they are willing to manufacture a crisis when needed.[141]

Forth: The Club of Rome began in 1968. A 1997 *National Review* article describes it as *"a small cadre of* obscure international bureaucrats" who "are hard at work devising a system of global governance."[142]

Fifth: The Trilateral Commission began in 1973 by David Rockefeller. Their logo is three intertwining sixes or 666. It was initially founded to encourage interaction and cooperation among the U.S., western Europe and Japan. Mentioned in its founding declaration is this quote, "Growing interdependence is a fact of life of the contemporary world. It **transcends** and influences national systems."

Note the word "transcends." Webster defines it as, "to be superior, surpass, excel." In other words, this interdependence is more important and is above the national sovereignty of any nation. According to Revelation 13:17, the antichrist will be in total control of the world's economic system. No one will be able to buy or sell without his mark. In order to "transcend" a nation's sovereignty, the need for a One World Government is implied.

Senator Barry Goldwater said this, "The Trilateral Commission is . . . intended to be the vehicle for multinational consolidation of the commercial and banking interests by seizing control of the political government of the United States."[143]

Six: The New Age Movement gained popularity in the Western World in the 1970s. David Spangler, a leader in the movement and listed in a 1975 document as a board member of the UN's Planetary Initiative and called a "Planetary Citizen," was told by his spirit guide to prepare for the New World Order and that their messiah, whose number is 666, will appear soon in bodily form.

He also said the following: *"No one will enter the New World Order unless he or she will make a pledge to worship Lucifer. No one will enter the New Age unless he will take a Luciferian Initiation."*[144]

So, we see that many of the "movers and shakers" of our world are part of one or more of these organizations. In 1975, thirty-two U.S. Senators and ninety-two U.S. Representatives signed a "Declaration of Independence" stating, *"we must bring forth a New World Order."* One can only imagine how much that number has grown!

Every year powerful men and women in governments around the world, including some of our own senators and congressmen, as well as powerful and influential men and women in the corporate world meet at the Bohemian Grove in California for a mock human sacrifice that takes place before a statue of an owl.

This occult ritual, called the "Cremation of Care" ceremony, was recorded several years ago by radio host, Alex Jones, along with a British filmmaker. They described it this way: *"Hooded figures of some of the world's wealthiest, most powerful men, including acting and former U.S. presidents such as George W. Bush, George H. W. Bush, Vice President Dick Cheney, and other participants gathered beneath a forty-foot stone owl surrounded by water. A child (or effigy) dubbed "Dull Care" was delivered by a ferryman on a small boat and placed on the altar before the owl, where it was burned as an offering for the purpose of magically alleviating the cares and concerns of those elitists making the sacrifice."*[145]

Is it any wonder why so many of our politicians, both Democrats and Republicans, are not working for the good of America? They, in fact, have another agenda. They are globalists and want a one world government. Not all globalists are Satanists, but many are and belong to one of the many secret societies connected to the Illuminati.

Like Nimrod's three-pronged power grab: political, financial and religious, the New Atlanteans will need to control all three as well. But these elites would do well to heed Jesus' caution, *"For what shall it profit a man, if he shall gain the whole world, and lose his own soul?"* (Mark 8:36)

The financial and political have been discussed above.

That leaves religion

It was Nimrod who successfully instituted a false religious system, Mystery Babylon, which encompassed forbidden occult knowledge as well as the worship of himself and his family (ancestor worship). They then went on to became "gods" in various cultures. Nimrod also introduced the worship of the twelve constellations. And all the above continue to plague us today.

The influence of Mystery Babylon is great and gaining inroads. In America and elsewhere, more and more churches no longer preach the full gospel. Instead, it's a watered-down version designed to offend no one. Some churches are doing "Clown Communions" in which the congregation and the pastor all dress up as clowns. Other churches are giving communion to their congregant's pets! There is even a "porn movie church" which shows an "R" rated film entitled, "Missionary Positions," under the guise of helping those addicted to porn. And who could believe there would ever be a nude church, where no one, including the pastor, wears clothes? But there is![146] God help us!

Doesn't 2 Timothy 4:3-4 warn of this? *"For the time will come when they will not endure sound doctrine; but after their own lusts shall they heap to themselves teachers, having itching ears; And they shall turn away their ears from the truth, and shall be turned unto fables."*

In addition, some are preaching "replacement theology" which claims that God is finished with Israel and has replaced her with the church. Replacement theology further claims that all Scriptures mentioning Israel really applies to the church. But try reading them that way. You'll have to twist yourself into knots to make the passages sound even remotely plausible. Instead of replacing Israel, God will install her as "head of nations" during the millennium.

In June 2011, the World Council of Churches met in Bolos Greece to discuss the growing number of Christians murdered at the hands of Muslims. And what was their conclusion? *Israel was responsible!* Furthermore, they declared the Jewish state a "sin"! If that weren't enough, they went on to say that Christians had the responsibility to resist this "offensive" Jewish existence.

Satan is still working hard to *crush* the Jews. His hatred for them is great. Remember, it was the Seed from their bloodline that sealed his doom. And it will be to their capital, Jerusalem, where that Seed, Jesus, will oust Satan's man, the antichrist, then rule and reign there Himself.

In conjunction with all these satanic efforts, the UN continues to actively promote "religious pluralism" which is another word for a one world religion. Working closely with them is the World Council of Churches.

Then there's the rise of Chrislam. According to a Christian Coalition newsletter, 300 churches have now added Islam to their Sunday school curriculum. It went on to say that on June 26, 2011, 500 U.S. churches in thirty-two states held "unity meetings" between Christianity and Islam, and placed the writings of the Quran and Bible on equal footing. They declared both books honor Jesus even though the prophet Jesus in the Quran has no resemblance to our Jesus. According to Islam, Jesus is **Not** the Son of God, **Not** virgin born, and **Never** died on the cross.

Muhammad Hisham Kabbani, Founder and Chairman of the Islamic Supreme Council of America, explains his Jesus this way (I paraphrase): Jesus will return with the Muslim Messiah, Mahdi, to establish a New World Order. When he does, he will confess that he never died on the cross, that it was all a fake.

He will further confess that while he was away, he discovered the truth of Islam. Then he will destroy all crosses and become the Mahdi's executioner of every man, woman and child who does not convert to Islam.

To say their prophet Jesus is the same as our Jesus of the Bible is utter blasphemy! So is trying to co-mingle Islam with Christianity.

But that's not all. Satan continues to make inroads in other areas. In June 2019, Carl Teichrib wrote an interesting article entitled, *Report from the Toronto Parliament of the World's Religion*. In it, he details his observations after attending that Parliament in November 2018. What was obvious was the sheer number of pagans represented. In fact, the very first day, according to Teichrib, was spent, *"reminding us how our loyalty and duty must be to Mother Earth."*

Teichrib witnessed native Americans calling on the spirits of their ancestors, Wiccan priestesses spouting their beliefs, pagan workshops, rants on the evils of "white, Euro-centric Christianity," a woman, claiming to be a Baptist minister, using Buddhist techniques to curse some of our leaders, and the overwhelming message that, "we are nobody's savior except our own." And all this was delivered in a tone of anger, hatred, and rancor.[147]

I fear this is just a preview of the future.

Sad to say, but our own government has become increasingly hostile to Christianity. One example was exposed on October 23, 2013, when Fox New posted an article to their website written by reporter Todd Sterns. The article covered a view held by some military higher-ups regarding evangelicals and the Tea Party, and how that view is creeping into the military at-large. Sterns wrote, *"Soldiers attending a pre-deployment briefing at Fort Hood say they were told that evangelical Christians and members of the Tea Party were a threat to the nation and that any soldier donating to those groups would be subjected to punishment under the Uniform Code of Military Justice."*[148] But praise God, President Trump is trying to reverse these things!

But why would our government do this?

Because, as we have seen, many in power are connected to secret societies and long for the *New Atlantis*. That means Christianity, one of the main obstacles preventing it, must be destroyed. And before the *New Atlantis* can fully emerge, paganism, socialism-communism, and the religion of material-ism must take its place.

And what is the religion of materialism? Dr. Michael Lake describes it in his book, *The Shinar Directive*, and lists these belief components:

- Man is just an animal
- There is no creator
- There is no god, except for yourself
- There are no absolutes
- There are no consequences for what we do[149]

So, what we see in all the above are the seeds of a one world religion. The world is getting ready for antichrist. It's interesting to note that the three major religions, Christianity, Judaism and Islam, are now all awaiting their messiah.

Next, the Catholic Church's role:

In 1948, the Vatican opposed the formation of the Jewish state while in 1962 their *Nostra Aetate* declared that the god of Islam and the God of Christianity were one and the same. Vatican II (1962-1965) went on to open its door for a One World Religion with its ecumenicalism. In 1982, Pope John Paul II had a prayer meeting in Assisi, Italy which included pagans and voodoo priests, and where he claimed that voodoo possessed *"truth and good, seeds of the Word."*[150]

Renowned Catholic Bishop, Fulton Sheen, said the false prophet would come from one of their own (a Catholic cardinal). But this was not a new fear. Martin Luther and Calvin believed it. So did John Knox, John Wesley, Charles Spurgeon, George Whitefield, and Jonathan Edwards. Dr. Henry Edward Cardinal Manning in 1861 predicted a crisis and apostasy in the Catholic Church.[151] Since then many others have come forward and sounded the same alarm, including Father E. Sylvester Berry in his book, *The Apocalypse of Saint John*, Father Herman Bernard Kramer in his, *"The Book of Destiny,"* Father John F. O'Connor, Father Alfred Kunz and Father Malachi Martin.[152]

Before he died, Father O'Connor said in a sermon that a, "Masonic Conspirator" would control the pope and assist the False Prophet in "deceiving the world's faithful into worshipping Antichrist."[153]

Could this be true?

"Prophecy of the Popes," a 12th century prophecy by an Irish Archbishop named Malachy O'Morgair, Papal Legate of Ireland and later called Saint Malachy, addresses this. In the prophecy he claims there would only be 112 more popes from his time forward until Jesus returned. And he describes each one. Pope Francis is number 112.

O'Morgair said of this pope, *"In the extreme persecution of the Holy Roman Church, there will sit Peter the Roman, who will nourish the sheep in many tribulations; when they are finished, the City of Seven Hills will be destroyed, and the terrible and fearsome Judge will judge his people."*[154] The prophecy indicates that this pope will be the end-times pope, the one who will oversee the apostate church spoken about in Revelation just before Jesus returns to earth as Judge and King of kings and Lord of lords.

Over the years, several Jesuits have worked hard to debunk the prophecy as a forgery. But despite the push-back, another Jesuit, Rene Thibaut, believed this prophecy to be true. A Belgium mathematician, professor, and scholar, Thibaut, in 1951, just a year before he died, published, *The Mysterious Prophecy of the Popes*, in which he details his calculations pointing to the year 2012 as the year the final pope would emerge on the scene.

I dislike date setting. God is in control. We are not. His timing is perfect and beyond our knowing. However, it is interesting to note that according to former Vatican Secretary of State, Cardinal Tarcisio Bertone, Pope Benedict XVI decided to resign in mid-2012,[155] paving the way for Pope Francis, the 266th pope and the 112th after St. Malachy's prediction. Jorge Mario Bergoglio took the name,

Francis, when he was elected to his position on March 3, 2013 and is the first **Jesuit** to ever wear the papal tiara.

Pope Benedict's resignation was unprecedented and the first in 600 years. Why he resigned is still a mystery. Perhaps his coverup and protection of pedophile priests had something to do with it. To his shame, he, as Cardinal Ratzinger, sent a secret decree telling Catholic bishops to *"put the Church's interests ahead of children."*[156]

How rotten is this house? Father Malachi Martin gives us an unsettling view. He was an eminent Catholic theologian, spoke seventeen languages, was a member of the Vatican Advisory Council and advisor to three popes. In addition, he was the Vatican's researcher on the Dead Sea Scrolls. He was also a Jesuit. Like Rene Thibaut before him, Martin believed in St. Malachy's prophecies and was greatly disturbed by the corruption in the church.[157]

His startling claim is this: An Illuminati-Masonic (Freemason) group had infiltrated the upper ranks of the Catholic Church and conspired to bring about a one world government. In his book, *Windswept House*, thinly disguised as fiction in order to protect sources and the innocent, Martin talks about "prominent clerics who worship Satan" and that "networks . . . had been established between certain clerical homosexual groups and Satanic covens." This lends even more insight into the world-wide cover-up of pedophile clerics by the church.

Martin also talked about a secret ceremony, which he called the, *"enthronement of Satan,"* and which took place at the Vatican in 1963 in order to ensure two outcomes: 1) Satan's control over Rome and 2) a demonically controlled end-time pope.[158] Pope Paul VI (pope from 1963-1978) called this ceremony, *"the smoke of Satan which has entered the Sanctuary."*[159]

Monsignor Luigi Marinelli backed this up in his 1999 book, *Gone with the Wind in the Vatican*, in which he talks of Catholic priests who have made pacts with Satanists and serve communion at Black Sabbath masses.[160] Then Archbishop Milingo, another senior cleric, also claimed that, *"high ranking Vatican officials were followers of Satan."*[161]

Martin died under "suspicious" circumstances in 1999 while working on another book connecting the Catholic Church with the New World Order.[162]

Malachi Martin knew the Jesuits. He was one of them and tried to expose their satanic cabal and activities in the Vatican. Though the Jesuit order began as a vehicle to defend the faith, they gradually shifted directions. Their main effort now is the promotion of Marxism and Liberation Theology. In his book, *The Jesuits: The Society of Jesus and the Betrayal of the Roman Catholic Church*, Martin claimed the order wanted to replace the Church's teaching with communist doctrine. Martin also claimed that Pope John XXIII made a secret agreement, called the Metz pact, with the USSR in order to have two Russian-Orthodox prelates participate in the Second Vatican Council.[163]

In a nutshell, the prevailing Jesuit belief is that, "the Scriptures are scientifically inaccurate obscurantisms (uncertainties)."[164]

Clearly Satan has had a foothold in the Vatican for centuries through members of the Freemasons and Illuminati. Pope Pius IX, serving as pope from 1846-1878, called it the *"Synagogue of Satan."* And in 1884, Pope Leo went so far as to issue an encyclical damning these Masonic efforts.[165]

Is Pope Francis the end-time pope? I don't know. But he has certainly made his share of unscriptural and even blasphemous statements. Here are just a few:

- Christians and Muslims worship the same God.[166]

- He called *"dangerous"* and *"harmful"* the belief that one *"can maintain a personal relationship with Jesus without the communion and mediation of the church."* Yes, we as a body need each other, but his statement contradicts Scripture that says any true relationship with our Lord, Jesus Christ, must be personal.

- Even Atheists can go to heaven.[167] Scripture clearly states that anyone not listed in the Lamb's Book of Life will be cast into the lake of fire (Revelation 3:5, Revelation 17:8, Revelation 20:15, Revelation 21:27). And how does one get into this book? Only by accepting Jesus as Savior. Jesus himself said in John 14:6, *"I am the way, the truth, the life: no man cometh unto the Father, but by me."* Does that mean Pope Francis is calling Jesus a liar?

- He said, *"proselytism is solemn nonsense, it makes no sense."*[168] This contradicts Jesus' command to, *"Go ye therefore, and teach all nations (the gospel) baptizing them in the name of the Father, and of the Son, and of the Holy Ghost."* (Matthew 28:19, Mark 16:15)

- He doesn't believe people will go to hell for all eternity. *"No one can be condemned forever, because that is not the logic of the Gospel!"*[169] Yet Jesus spoke of hell and eternal damnation many times (Mark 9:43-48, Matthew 10:28, Mark 3:29, Luke 12:5, Hebrews 6:2, Jude 7, Revelation 1:18).

- He called Italian abortion advocate, Emma Bonino, a "forgotten great." Bonino championed the legalization of abortion, as well as decriminalization of recreational drugs, homosexual marriage, euthanasia, and graphic sex education.[170]

The Vatican showed its true colors and made its objectives clear in 2011 when it published, *Toward Reforming the International Financial and Monetary Systems in the context of a Global Public Authority*, which espoused the same goals as those of the New World Order, declaring the need for individuals and nations to surrender their rights and authority in order to achieve *"global civil and economic security."*

And how was this to be accomplished? Their answer: *"at the cost of a gradual balance transfer of a part of each nation's powers to a world authority and to regional authorities."*[171] Sounds like the One World Government!

Jesus said you will know them by their fruits and that good trees produce good fruit and bad trees produce evil fruit (Matthew 7:16-18). As we see corruption unfold in politics, religion, and the financial arena, it's easy to spot the bad fruit. And it's all too clear who is responsible.

And yes, for a season, Satan and his crowd will have their way. But God always gets the last laugh.

"Why do the heathen rage, and the people imagine a vain thing? The kings of the earth set themselves, and the rulers take counsel together, against the LORD, and against his anointed, saying, Let us break their bands asunder, and cast away their cords from us. He that sitteth in the heavens shall laugh: the LORD shall have them in derision." Psalms 2:1-4

"Order Out of Chaos"

The New World Order's motto: "order out of chaos" is telling. It helps explain why Rohm Emanuel said, "Never let a good crisis go to waste." And why Hillary Clinton said something similar in March 2009. Chaos is just another word for crisis. And a crisis or chaos allows those in power to step in and initiate things they would not normally be able to do. It's the perfect excuse for eroding more and more of our personal freedoms.

But what happens if there is no crisis? Well, then, manufacture one! And climate change is one of their best. It's the new religion of the elites, and like all false religions, it's based on a hoax, a false premise. For the true devotees it's really a worship of the ancient goddess, Gaia, the worship of mother earth. For the elites, it's something else entirely.

Does that mean I think climate change is a hoax?

Yes.

Before you throw the book against the wall, let me explain. First off, the term "climate change" is utterly meaningless. Why? Because the climate is always changing. Today it is windy, tomorrow sunny, the next day humid and overcast. Summer is different than Spring, Fall is different than Winter. You get the idea. So, why all this hoopla about our changing climate?

Some background:

It was initially called "global warming." The only problem was that scientists couldn't prove the earth had warmed to any significant degree. In 2013, even the UN's Intergovernmental Panel on Climate Change admitted the earth had not warmed in fifteen years.[172]

Professor Wilfred Beckerman, member of the British Royal Commission on Environmental Pollution and former advocate of global warming said, *"Within a few months of looking at the statistical data, I realized that most of my concerns about the environment were based on false information and scare stories."*[173]

Fred Singer, an atmospheric physicist claims that global warming is essentially a myth. Its evidence consists of questionable computer models that are unable to even predict past cooling and warming events. And the assertions of global warming advocates are fueled by those who stand to gain monetarily from the very actions they claim will remedy the bogus problem.[174]

Singer also said, *"Why should we devote our scare resources to what is essentially a non-problem . . . Yet politicians and the elites throughout much of the world prefer to squander our limited resources to fashionable issues, rather than concentrate on real problems."*[175]

But doesn't Al Core and others say climate change is a "settled issue" and that there's no more need for debate; that all the scientific evidence is in? Yes, but these statements are meant to shut down honest discussion. And yes, many scientists have come on board to tout this latest hoax.

If that's true, why would scientists risk their reputation by boarding a derailed train? Because most scientists need grants in order to do their research. And these grants come from government, universities, and philanthropic organizations. And most grants are award to those who are researching the current "thing" — the hot topic of the day. So, it's in the best interest of said scientists to climb on board otherwise, in many cases, no grant money, no income, no way to continue their independent research. Sad to say, many will manipulate their findings in order to keep their funding or gain additional ones.

Edith Efron, in her book, *The Apocalyptics*, said, *"Normally, scientific research leads to scientific conclusions, not to metaphysical manifestos, prophetic outbursts, utopian reorganizations of society, and political positions, let alone to a set of internationalist positions on the redistribution of wealth from rich to poor nations, which are clearly identifiable as positions taken by the far left portion of the political spectrum."*[176]

Groups like the Club of Rome often hold critical press conferences to announce dire "scientific" findings before others in the scientific community can review the data on which the claims are based.[177] The prevailing MO is to create an ecological annihilation scenario requiring immediate attention as well as some government intervention.

Regarding this, Peter Rogers, Harvard University researcher said, *"Because everyone else is crying 'crisis,' responsible scientists are forced to join the chorus or risk losing their research programs."*[178] How sad!

In 1991, the Club of Rome made this statement regarding environmental issues: *"Never in the course of history has humankind been faced with so many threats and dangers,"*[179] The Club even recommended the need for an Environmental Security Council.[180] But it looks like the UN has that covered now. In June 2015, the UN Security Council met to "better identify the inter-connected threats to international peace and security related to Climate Change."[181]

That should raise some red flags. It shows the serious intent of the elites. Now that the UN has linked climate change with global security, what kind of things can they propose in the interest of keeping us "safe"? I suspect the sky is the limit.

In the 70s the current "thing" or hot topic was the coming of a new ice age. That's right. A new ice age. In 1975, The National Academy of Sciences warned that earth might be "on the brink of a full-blown Great Ice Age."[182] So, it wasn't to be just another ice age, but a "Great Ice Age." Many of the top scientists ran with it. And magazines like *Science Digest* were full of their articles.

But the secular news also carried the banner. *Newsweek* and *The Chicago Tribune* as well as periodicals like *National Geographic* all confessed the same thing. Even *Time* did a feature article enumerating the coming disasters the cold weather could bring.[183] Here is the type of rhetoric heard in many quarters: *"The threat of a new ice age must now stand alongside nuclear war as a likely source of wholesale death and misery for mankind."*[184]

Many believers in global cooling and their proteges are now advocates of global warming. As global coolers, they once believed reduced temperatures would cause places like India and the U.S. Midwest to experience draughts. Now, as global warmers they are saying the same thing, that draughts will be seen in these same areas. The solution is also the same: drastic and immediate actions which may necessitate the redistribution of wealth, loss of national sovereignty as well as loss of free markets and property rights.[185]

Remember, groups like The Club of Rome and almost all major news outlets belong to or are part of one or more of the secret societies. And their interest is not in the climate but in amassing power and ushering in the New World Order.

Other Myths:

So, we've already seen a globalist myth fade, that of a coming ice age. Were there others? Yes. The environmentalists have been predicting calamities for years. And none have materialized. In the 1970s, along with the "ice age" scare, the major predictions were: massive famines due to overpopulation in places like India, topsoil erosion, depletion of the ozone layer and deforestation.

Let's take a quick look at each:

Massive Famines: By 1971, India was self-sufficient regarding their food supply. And in the 1980s they began exporting grain to Russia.[186] And in the past twenty years, developing countries have increased their grain production through higher yields rather than expanding their planting areas. In addition, the Soil Conservation Services "estimates that topsoil regenerates at five tons per acre per year." While Pierre Crosson, soil expert for the environmental organization, *Resources for the Future*," cites studies showing regeneration rates of twelve to sixty tons (per acre) per year are not uncommon."[187] Indeed, most of the world's famines have been caused by war and the displaced people unable to plant crops.

Depletion of ozone layer: This so-called "crisis" began in 1974 by chemist Sherwood Rowland and Mario Molina at the University of California at Irvine. They claimed that chlorofluorocarbons could deplete the earth's ozone layer. Rowland even jokingly told his wife, *"looks like the end of the world."* Then in 1985 a British science journal, *Nature*, expanded on this by talking about the "hole in the ozone layer above the Antarctic." And suddenly the crisis went mainstream.[188]

In a February 1992 press conference, NASA scientists joined the chorus by warning that an ozone hole may be opening over America, endangering its citizens with potentially harmful ultraviolet sunlight. That same month, *Time* featured a story declaring that "danger is shining through the sky."

A month later the danger disappeared when in March, meteorologists Dirk De Muer and his team at the Belgian Meteorological Institute found that instruments in measuring ozone "had mistaken reductions in atmospheric sulfur dioxide for declines in global ozone" and "that once the sulfur dioxide trends are taken into account, there appears to be a small **upward** trend in global ozone."[189] You mean an **increase** and not a decrease?

Then in April 30, 1992, NASA acknowledged that a "large arctic ozone depletion had been averted." Why the hyperbole and scare tactics? It seems the initial February press conference was scheduled around their new budget request for their climate change program.[190] And what better way to insure those funds than a looming crisis?

Deforestation: The premise was that if environmentalists didn't stop logging, ranching and mining, the forests would die, and probably everything else. And don't forget about acid rain. That was certain to be a forest killer. But though it did hurt some lakes, it did not damage forests. At the same time the environmentalists were claiming that all these factors were shrinking our forests, forests world-wide actually **increased** .85% from 1950 to 1994.[191]

Our federal forests were set aside for the purpose of furnishing "a continuous supply of timber for the use and necessities of citizens of the United States."[192] That was before the Sierra Club decided to work for a "Zero Cut" policy on federal lands and filed a lawsuit in 1989 regarding the Spotted Owl and the Endangered Species Act. To their delight, in June 1990, the ruling came down in their favor, virtually shutting down federal harvesting of timber and causing an eventual loss of 22,654 jobs.[193]

After that, the government began buying up private land. According to Ron Arnold, author of *Undue Influence*, "*If some bureaucrat draws a line on a national park map and your property happens to be inside the line, you become an 'inholder,' subject to federal authority, and you are about to live in interesting times.*"[194] Currently, the U.S. government owns one-third of America's land.

Loggers have long endured sabotage such as tree spiking which destroys their saws, having their brake lines cut and shotguns rigged with fishing lines across their paths. Many have been injured all because the elites think they know better than we and have declared themselves saviors of the planet. An environmental advocate, in his letter to the *New York Times* editor, declared environmentalists to be *"the lay priests of a different gospel that can help save us."*[195] And historian Anna Bramwell said, *"Ecologists are the saved"* and believe they are *"better able to plan man, space, and the environment than existing institutions."*[196]

All this hubris has a cost. And it's costing Oregon and California big time where mining operations have been seriously curtailed. Also, their fires in recent years have become more powerful and destructive, costing millions if not billions of dollars, not to mention lives. While there are many contributing factors that cause these fires such as dry weather conditions, the Santa Anna winds, etcetera, the environmentalists must also shoulder blame.

Why?

Because among the many reasons they cited for hamstringing the logging industry, the one they failed to mention was drugs. Marijuana in particular. It seems that one of the reasons they didn't want loggers traipsing in the woods was because of their marijuana farms.

In 1983 James Corlett, manager of the Oregon Forest Protection Association, warned loggers not to interfere "with marijuana plantations discovered on private land or guerrilla plantations in national forests."[197]

And Doug Plumley, head of a road construction crew in the area, "knew that a new breed of heavily armed seasonal marijuana growers from San Francisco had virtually taken over the national forests just across the county line in Northern California." This group was so violent that even law enforcement didn't dare go into the Six Rivers or the Shasta-Trinity National Forests.[198]

As a result, forests aren't being thinned properly nor dead vegetation removed, creating plenty of fuel for fires to grow, leap and consume more than they should.

It's clear that while many environmentalists are sincere and non-violent, many are not. Their history reveals a trail of terror, intimidation, violence and scare tactics. In 1994 the Gaia Liberation Front advocated for the "total eradication of all humans as the only way to save nature."[199] Radical environmentalists are not above sending parcel bombs, letters containing poisoned razor blades, damaging private property or harassing and threatening those who stand in their way. And this all while beating the constant drum of earth's impending doom.

Environmentalist, Bill McKibben, in his book, *The End of Nature*, reveals their underlining method. *"The ecological movement has always had its greatest success in convincing people that we are threatened by some looming problem."*[200]

Wildavsky, in his *Radical Egalitarianism*, says it even better: *"bring all the dangers of the future into the present, hold them over people, and say the most terrible things will happen unless (the environmentalists') views are accepted. If we are not freezing to death from nuclear winter, for instance, then the greenhouse effect is going to fry us to a crisp. The solution, of course, will be local, state, national, international, and intergalactic regulations to prevent these awful things from happening."*[201]

These tactics are not new. They have existed for ages and have been employed by people with agendas seeking power. Journalist, satirist, and cultural critic, H.L. Mencken (1880-1956) understood that when he said, *"The whole aim of practical politics is to keep the populace alarmed (and hence clamorous to lead them to safety) by menacing it with an endless series of hobgoblins, all of them imaginary."*[202]

There are at least 450 national environmental organization plus many local ones promoting their causes. And "without calamities to combat, they have no reason to exist."[203]

As a result, there is an "iron" coalition of money, scientists, lawyers, lobbyists and politicians that make it all work. Add that to the perks and salaries paid to the staff of these environmental organizations, it becomes clear that this cabal isn't going away any time soon.[204] And the only thing that keeps them relevant is a crisis.

Also revealing is the fact that the environmental movement contains many elements of Marxism. Paul Johnson in his book, *The Enemies of Society*, writes that the global environmental crisis is the very vehicle that will destroy capitalism.[205] I thought the environmentalists just wanted to save the planet.

But there are other similarities between this movement and Communism. While Marxists wanted to create a "New Soviet Man," radical environmentalists want to create a "New Ecological

Person."[206] Like Marxists, radical environmentalists want more government control, shared resources (read, no more private poverty) social justice, and a revolution of sorts that fundamentally changes minds, laws, and religious beliefs.

Back to global warming:

Unfortunately for global warming enthusiasts, the scientific data stubbornly refused to support their theory. Then other scientists spilled the beans by saying that earth's temperature was largely affected by solar flares, meaning the solar minimum and solar maximum. And that these flares, these fiery discharges from the sun, was a cyclical event, with each lasting about twelve years. When in the cycle of solar minimum, the earth isn't as hot. When it changes to a solar maximum, warmer temperatures ensue. A few years ago we entered the cycle of solar maximum, so yes, our weather should get warmer, just in time for climate advocates to use it in support of their theory without mentioning the actual cause.

But what about greenhouse gas. Surely that's real?

Yes, the greenhouse gas effect is real but has been incredibly exaggerated. Human influence as well as carbon emissions have only a miniscule effect on the environment. Predictions of impact to agriculture, rising sea levels, rise in human health issues, and extreme weather have never materialized. In fact, so far not one dire prediction of the last fifty years has come to pass.

So why push it? Especially since it will cost a fortune. In 2010, they estimated the cost of implementing the Kyoto Protocol, the plan to combat global warming, to be $346 billion a year at a total cost of about $5 trillion.[207] Yet, if the Kyoto Protocols were to be implemented, it was predicted that by the year 2100 the reduction in global temperatures would be a mere .03° Celsius![208] It doesn't make sense. Even Richard Lindzen, noted MIT climatologist, takes issue with what the computer climate models are pumping out. He terms it, "garbage in, garbage out."[209] Only 17% of the scientists with the Institute of Science, Technology and Media believe global warming has begun, with a whopping 53% of their scientists believing that no global warming has occurred. The rest are undecided.[210] But here's the kicker: some scientists believe that "increase atmospheric CO_2 might trigger a new **ice age**."[211] *What?* Aren't CO_2 emissions supposed to make everything hotter?

It's obvious that scientists are all over the place on this subject. Some are courageous enough to admit it. Others are not. NASA's Roy Spencer admits that scientists who don't *"jump on the environmental bandwagon"* regarding global warming, will be ostracized by their peers.[211]

So, the above "inconvenient truth" demanded a redo. But what? Simple. Switch the term "global warming" to the nebulous phrase of "climate change." Now there's a term broad enough to cover countless issues. It was the gargantuan umbrella they needed. Facts were no longer important. Evidence didn't matter. Now, everything and anything could be attributed to affecting our climate, even the flatulence of cows. And only one thing could prevent this scourge. More government control!

Ah, now we're getting to the heart of it. The climate change scare is not about our climate at all. It's about control. It's about redistribution of wealth. It's about taking money from the industrialized nations, the evil nations that have the largest carbon footprint and taxing them with a "carbon tax" then giving that money to less developed nations that didn't use as much energy. It's interesting to note that most of these less developed nations have histories of corruption. So why would anyone think that giving them money, money from nations that tried to curb their own corruption, though not always success-fully, and whose people thrived and created jobs and factories and stores and vehicles, would not end up where it always has, in the secret bank accounts of despots?

This umbrella is the perfect means to control people and governments world-wide. Under it, the elites can tell people what cars to drive, what kind of houses to live in, what food they can eat, and even what kind of straws they can use! A socialist Utopia. Now, at last, the elites, on a global scale, can dictate what kind of society will be allowed to thrive on planet earth. And based on history, it will be two-tiered: the elites with the rest of us becoming the servants/slaves, because that's what socialism eventually boils everything down to.

But aren't we supposed to be good stewards of the earth? Yes. God has instructed us to take care of our planet and we should. We should intelligently protect and conserve our natural resources while curtailing pollution. But that's a far cry from what "climate change" is all about. As previously stated, it's about power.

One last element needs to be addressed—the connection between climate change and religion. Some big organizations have courted favor with the Christian sector in order to further their agenda. One such example is *Christianity Today* who was given $135,000 by the Pew Charitable Trusts to write about "population and consumption issues" and "global stewardship."[212]

But it's a bit bizarre since Christians are hardly at the forefront of this movement while New Agers and Gaia worshippers are. Both have pagan roots. Gaia or "Mother Earth" worshippers credit the earth with giving life. Nature is personified and man is seen as the destroyer of that nature, the enemy. For that reason, man must be restrained by strict limits and laws, hence, the need for a large bureaucracy, rules and regulations. Their hubris makes them believe they can, if given enough power, control our climate.

The irony is that our planet will one day become unbearably hot, and many of the environmentalists' dire predictions will come true. But it won't be by the hand of man or from cows or SUVs but by the hand of God, Himself, when He judges the earth during the seven-year Tribulation. *"And men were scorched with great heat, and blasphemed the name of God, which hath* **power** *over the plagues; and they repented not to give him glory."* (Revelation 16:9)

God is not mocked. He will have the last say. When men try to usurp Him or worship the creation rather than the Creator, judgment is bound to fall. But until then, God promises there will be seedtime and harvest, in other words, we will continue to experience the four seasons. *"While the earth remaineth, seedtime and harvest, and cold and heat, and summer and winter, and day and night shall not cease."* Genesis 8:22

Ye shall be as gods—Take Two

There really isn't anything new. King Solomon was right when he made that claim in Ecclesiastes 1:9. And he was right when he said what was done will be done again. History does tend to repeat itself.

Does that mean because fallen angels were on earth cohabitating with women and producing offspring during Noah and Lot's day, and because Jesus said that the last days would be like the days of Noah and Lot, that it will happen again? Will fallen angels really return to earth and cohabitate with women?

Yes, they will return to earth and have already done so. And no, they will not cohabitate with women.

Before I go into this let me sidetrack and talk about Nazi Germany. Hitler and virtually everyone in the SS had deep ties to the occult. That included many of their scientists who were Nazis as well as SS officers. It's common knowledge that Germany was well advanced in rocketry and jet propulsion, and even experimented with saucer-like aircraft. Many of these scientists claimed they were aided in their technical advances by "entities." Not surprising. If you dabble in the occult, sooner or later you'll begin hearing from "entities."

The Cutting Edge Studios' documentary, *Blood Sacrifice—Cleansing the Soil for the Aryan Antichrist*, reveals how the ashes of those killed in concentration camps were used in occult rituals to cleanse the land of Christianity.[213]

In addition, Hitler tried to collect religious artifacts because he believed they contained supernatural power. His goal was to create a state occult religion that would replace Christianity.[214]

After the war, the Allied Nations, desiring the German technology as well as their acquired knowledge in other fields, split up the scientists. The U.S., under Operation Paperclip, secretly and illegally brought in numerous Nazi scientists.[215] These scientists went on to fill high places in biology, chemistry, medicine, mathematics and rocketry, including our NASA space program, which was headed by German scientist Warner Von Braun.[216] Many of these scientists also brought their occult beliefs with them making some of these disciplines godless and rooted in evil.

As a result of this occult influence, many scientists, world-wide, have no fear of God and are heavily involved in the satanic transhumanist movement—the remaking of mankind. And humanity 2.0 is to be achieved by mixing human DNA with animal or even plant DNA and artificial intelligence.

One of Obama's first acts as president in 2009 was to remove Bush's restrictions on stem cell research. Now, there are no barriers left on human DNA experimentations. The sky is the limit. Finally, transhumanists can go full-bore in implementing their agenda.

These scientists have already created kits that can modify human DNA and make a human into something else, something "other." The kit is called CRISPR-Cas9, short for, "clusters of regularly interspaced short palindromic repeats." Simply put, it's the altering of DNA to modify gene function. It's playing god. And now every person on earth can play god, too, because CRISPR has become available as a home-do-it-yourself-kit. It comes in a small box with about four or five pre-filled injectable syringes which, when they are administered in a specific sequence, can alter DNA. Right now, it's being touted as something good because it can possibly target serious diseases such as Alzheimer's, leukemia, and cancer.[217] But that's how it always starts. Satan is no dummy. Get the foot in the door then come out with the real agenda, which is to corrupt mankind, change him into something detestable to the Creator.

This is exactly what the fallen angels did in ancient times. They created hybrid humans by comingling their seed with women and by comingling the seed of animals and plants with human DNA. Now scientists are offering us the same thing, the co-mingling of humans, plants, animals, as well as something new—machines. It's a virtual smorgas-bord of possibilities. Or so they claim.

In Genesis, God commanded that seed was to **produce after its kind** and not be mixed. Changing the genetic code of any living creature is an insult to God and an affront to the perfection of His creation. Even so, this satanic tinkering of the human genome is now occurring unabated in labs around the world. Already a lab in Great Britain claims to have created a chimera, a totally new species that is part human and part animal, but claims to have destroyed it. If this is what they are admitting openly, one can only imagine what is going on in secret!

As labs around the world change what it means to be a human or an animal, new laws will be needed. In 2006 the Department of Health commissioned Case Law School to create guidelines concerning "trans-humans" and "bioethics." Just what will the rights of a hybrid man-animal be? Did they grapple with questions like, "Can it have citizenship?" "Can it marry?" One can only guess. But not a half dozen years later, Case School of Medicine professor, Mazwell Mehlman, received almost a million dollars to "develop standards for test on human subjects in research that involves the use of genetic technologies to enhance 'normal individuals'."[218]

Joseph Infranco, lawyer for the Alliance Defense Fund, said, *"We are well beyond the science fiction of H.G. Wells' tormented hybrids in the Island of Doctor Moreau. We are in the time where scientists are seriously contemplating the creation of human-animal hybrids."*[219]

Leon Kass, former chairman of the President's Council on Bioethics from 2001-2005, confirms this. *"Human nature itself lies on the operation table, ready for alteration, for eugenic and psychic 'enhancement,' for wholesale redesign. In leading laboratories, academic and industrial, new creators are confidently amassing their powers and quietly honing their skills, while on the street their evangelists (transhumanists) are zealously prophesying a posthuman future. For anyone who cares about preserving our humanity, the time has come for paying attention."*[220]

Even the government has joined the effort. JASON, the highest think-tank of the Pentagon, believing that creating Human 2.0 is the next arms race, said that if they didn't enter the bio-tech war soon it would be too late, and that they needed to create a new species of man for the battlefield. In the Pentagon's 2011 budget, millions were set aside to redesign human DNA in order to create super battlefield soldiers.[221] Does that mean they will be willing to cross humans with animals to create, for example, a man with eagle's eyes, or with the skin of an armadillo? It looks that way.

DARPA, the Pentagons' Defense Advanced Research Projects Agency, with a budget of $2 billion a year, has become "the world's largest funder of 'gene driven' research."[222] In 2013, DARPA requested a bid for Project ST13B-001, which involved "mammalian genome engineering," in other words, mixing animal and human DNA.[223]

DARPA also employs occult practices. Their wheelhouse includes telepathy, remote viewing (a form of astral projection) and psychic spying. And it's well ahead of the curve since it has been trying to develop "super soldiers" since the 1960s when they employed such techniques as "genetic enhancements, implants, drugs, neuroscience, computer technologies, and chips."[224] Again, it's not hard to guess that they have continued where the Nazis left off.

Long before this, Dr. Kass, warned that, *"All of the boundaries are up for grabs. All of the boundaries that have defined us as human beings, boundaries between a human being and an animal and between a human being and a super human being or a **god**."*

And there it is. The bottom line. Transhumanists want a Utopia without God. In fact, they want to be god. An avatar is defined as an artificial body having the consciousness of a person. In Hinduism, it "was the form a god took when it went from heaven to earth."[225] It appears that these scientists are attempting reverse engineering, making humans into gods. And some big companies are beginning to embrace their ideas.

Their stated goal:

What transhumanists admit they want is to drastically increase human lifespan as well as increase human intelligence, strength and ability. In other words, they want to create a "super race." They view this as the "next step in evolution" and are willing to do just about anything to achieve it.

In many respects, transhumanism continues where the U.S. and Hitler's 1900s eugenics programs left off. Nietzsche's idea of the *Ubermensch* or Superman captivated Hitler's imagination and spurred Nazi efforts to create an entire race of superior humans. These attempts began in the 1930s and continued throughout World War II. It's not surprising, then, that when Nazis scientists were smuggled into other countries, they and their proteges continued this work.

Nick Bostrom, professor at Oxford and a proponent of transhumanism, makes their position clear, *"Transhumanists view human nature as a work-in-progress, a half-baked beginning that we can learn to remold in desirable ways. Current humanity need not be the endpoint of evolution. Transhumanists hope that by responsible use of science, technology, and other rational means we shall eventually manage to become post-human beings with vastly greater capacities than present human beings have."*[226]

But surely their agenda is good? Or at least not **all** bad? I'll let the words of Richard Seed, physicist and cloning advocate, speak for themselves. *"We are going to become gods, period. If you don't like it, get off. You don't have to contribute, you don't have to participate but if you are going to interfere with me becoming a god, you're going to have trouble. There'll be warfare."*[227]

Zoltan Istvon, Former Presidential Candidate for the Transhumanist Party, simplifies it by saying,

"Transhumanism's number one goal is to not die and to become godlike through technology."[228]

Stephen Quayle, in his book, *Angel Wars*, believes that computer scientist and Google's Director of Engineering, Ray Kurzweil, as well as other proponents of the Singularity movement "are offering godhood to those who accept their new religion. Not simply godhood mind you, but 'master of the universe 'godhood.'"[229]

And artificial intelligence researcher, Alexander Chislenko says, *"It's morphic freedom. Humans as we know and love them will cease to exist in a few generations."*[230]

What arrogance to believe they can improve on God's design! To say this movement has Satan's fingerprints all over it is an understatement. It blatantly defies God and His natural law. It is just another battle in the war between the "seed of the woman" and the "seed of the serpent" as foretold in Genesis 3:15.

Thankfully, there are some raising the alarm. In their 2012 paper entitled, *"Human Enhancement and the Future of Work,"* the Academy of Medical Sciences voiced their concern over the new "hybrid age" and the "arrival of a new form of man" which among other characteristics could have "serpentine qualities" enabling them to "detect infrared wavelengths."[231] Oh brother! That doesn't sound like anything I'd like to have!

Some Background:

The two men credited with popularizing the concept of transhumanism are Hans Moravec and Ken Warwick. Moravec is a futurist who believes that by 2045 knowledge transfer from a human to an artificial brain is achievable thus allowing humans to become "eternal." The second man, UK Professor of Cybernetics, Kevin Warwick, achieved fame by "interfacing computer systems with the human nervous system."[232]

How they plan to achieve it:

What devices will be and are already being used? Well, as in most things Satan has influenced, it started out small and was in a form most people found acceptable like somatic cell gene therapy which injects healthy genic material into patients with various diseases, like Huntington's. Then it progressed to germline therapy which alters so called "defective" genes. The problem is the "alteration" can't be reversed and can be passed on to future generations. And who knows the ramifications or unintended consequences of that?

Then came the biggie, genetic enhancement therapy. This includes altering one's existing DNA by mixing it with plants or animals or both, creating a GMO, a Genetically Modified Organism or Human 2.0. The next step: human cloning for spare parts.

Ever heard of "Designer Baby Clinics"? Great Britain opened them in 2006 where human embryos were examined and if they didn't measure up, were destroyed. Only those not found "defective" or "inferior" were used for in vitro fertilization.[233] What's next? Modifying your baby's eye color? His/her nose, hair, height, etcetera? No, that's already being done!

What about three-parent babies? Believe it or not, this happened in 2016 through spindle nuclear transfer, resulting in a baby being born with the DNA of three people.[234]

Here are just a few other experiments that have been or are currently being done: creating human-pig embryos, cross species experiments, cloning extinct or endangered species, and homosexual reproduction. Regarding human-pig experiments, to their shame, scientists, in 2017, "created the first human-pig hybrid for the purpose of one day growing human organs inside these hybrids to use for transplants."[235]

Other such experiments include 1) adding a silk gene to goats 2) injecting mice with a bovine growth hormone gene to create a "super mouse" 3) pigs with mice DNA[236] 4) mice with human brains and 5) fusing human cells with rabbit eggs[237] And this is just the tip of the iceberg!

Many believe that scientists are also mixing human DNA with DNA extracted from bones of the giant Nephilim and Rephaim. To create what? A new race of demonic giants? Since I currently don't have a solid reference to cite, I'll just chalk it up to speculation. But the idea is not that far-fetched. Remember all those bones hidden away by the Smithsonian? That cache would certainly provide scientists with plenty of Nephilim and Rephaim DNA to work with.

And here's some other interesting facts: In 2014, traces of non-human DNA, not matching any known species in the GenBank, was found in the nuclear DNA of several human test subjects.[238] This strange mitochondrial DNA, Haplogroup X, is found in people groups worldwide including numerous Native American tribes.[239] It's interesting that some of these tribes claim kinship with the fallen ones. Could this strange DNA be that of the Nephilim or Rephaim? If so, perhaps that explains our government's effort to take control of some of their burial grounds and sacred sites.

But whatever these scientists are doing in their secret labs, the bottom line remains the same. Much of their knowledge is based on fallen angel technology or forbidden occult knowledge given to man illegally. The fallen angels don't have to cohabitate with women anymore in order to corrupt the human genome. They have enlisted man to do it for them. And in creating man in his own image, man can do away with God and make himself creator.

The sad thing is that we now have a generation so enamored with technology that many would be willing and even thrilled to be augmented by it.

What will this new posthuman world look like?

It's quite frightening if you listen to what the adherents are saying.

"The new species or 'posthuman' will likely view the old 'normal' humans as inferior, even savages, and fit for

slavery or slaughter." George Annas, Professor at Boston University[240]

Author Noboru Kawazoe gives us additional insight into these new "superior" humans. *"After several decades, with the rapid progress of communication technology, every one will have a 'brain wave receiver' in his ear, which conveys directly and exactly what other people think about him and vice versa. What I think will be known by all the people. There is no more individual consciousness, only the will of mankind as a whole"*[241]

Would you be surprised to learn that, "there are already those in the Transhuman movement calling for concentrations camps for those who fail to make the transition"?[242]

Another desired goal is the depopulation of the world. Apparently, it must be drastically decreased before Utopia can be realized.

Famous oceanographer, Jacques Cousteau (1910-1997) said in 1991, *"In order to stabilize world population, we must eliminate 350,000 people per day."*[243] Ah, but who gets to decide who those 350,000 are? The elites, I imagine.

David Brower, first Executive Direct of the Sierra Club, apparently agrees with depopulation and has come up with a plan. *"Childbearing (should be) a punishable crime against society, unless the parents hold a government license . . . All potential parents (should be) required to use contraceptive chemicals, the government issuing antidotes to citizens chosen for childbearing."*[244]

Wow! Concentrations camps, forced sterilization, strict government control—it's all beginning to sound a lot like Nazi Germany!

Francis Crick, Nobel Prize winning British molecular biologist and co-discoverer of DNA (1916-2004) actually said that babies are "non-human" and that it was reasonable for doctors and parents to take as long as three days after the birth to determine if they are "worth keeping."[245] What a horrifying thought! He was advocating nothing less than infanticide—*murder*!

Remember the Club of Rome, one of the elite societies trying to bring about the *New Atlantis*? Here's what they say in their *Goals for Mankind*, "the resultant ideal sustainable population is hence more than 500 million but less than one billion."[246]

Let that sink in. The very elites that control almost everything, believe that only about 500 million to one billion people should be allowed to populate the

Sylvia Bambola

earth. According to the internet, as of April 2019, the earth's population was 7.7 billion. That means there are at least 6.7 billion undesirable people currently living. I wonder how they plan to get rid of them?

Dr. Eric Pianka, a University of Texas Evolutionary Ecologist, has a few ideas: *"AIDS is not an efficient killer . . . it is too slow. My favorite candidate for eliminating 90 percent of the world's population is airborne Ebola because it is both highly lethal and it kills in days, instead of years. . . We've got airborne 90 percent mortality in humans. Killing humans. Think about that . . . You know the bird flu's good too. For everyone who survives, he will have to bury nine."*[247]

And Bilderberg member and former Secretary of State, Henry Kissinger, makes these disturbing pronouncements: *"Depopulation should be the highest priority of foreign policy towards the third world."* And *"world population needs to be decreased by 50%."*[248]

Then there's Mikhail Gorbachev, last general secretary of the Soviet Union, who said, *"We must speak more clearly about sexuality, contraception, about abortion, about values that control population, because the ecological crisis, in short, is the population crisis. Cut the population by 90% and there aren't enough people left to do a great deal of ecological damage."*[249]

Is that why so many big names are connected to programs that currently provide birth control and promote abortion in third world countries? You bet!

In addition, both Tesla (1856-1943, engineer and scientist who designed the AC electric system) and Elon Musk (CEO of SpaceX) declared that in the future only people who are cyborgs, who are connected to artificial intelligence, will be relevant.[250]

So, the picture becomes clear. This is their idea of Utopia: a depopulated earth, super humans who will live forever and be masters over the rest—those "inferior authentic humans"—and all operating in the same or "hive collective" mind. The population will be three tiered: the elite, the worker class and the military or police force. But that doesn't sound much like Utopia to me. At least not a Utopia I'd be interested in. But it does please Satan, the hater of mankind. He now has people who want to destroy or eliminate 50% to 90% of the human race! It is a Luciferin plan, plain and simple. And the elites, those members of secret societies, are working hard to ensure this agenda becomes a reality.

What also becomes clear is why it was so important to introduce the theory of evolution and why Satan has worked so hard to keep it mainstream as well as in the forefront of our schools and universities, and why it was important to silence all debate. If there is no Creator and we have all crawled out of the slime pit and evolved, then what's wrong with giving evolution a helping hand through science and technology? What these elitists don't realize is that they are playing into Satan's hands and are ensuring their own demise and that of their offspring.

Even Stephen Hawking predicts that AI could be the "end of the human race."[251] Already it has infiltrated our lives. Everything from car manufacturers to the healthcare system uses some form of it. It's now even in our homes. What is currently billed as something to help make our lives easier can just as quickly turn into a monitoring agent, able to spy on our every word and action. AI has already been installed in smart phones and there are plans to weaponize it for military purposes. Also underway is the effort to teach AI to think like humans and predict our actions. Remember, the antichrist will be able to rule worldwide because of all this new technology. What man may have initially meant for good will ultimately be used for evil by Satan.

Already the concept of human and robot babies is being explored. Artificial intelligence researcher, Dr. David Levy, believes that "cells can be manipulated to create a baby with human and robot DNA."[252]

Not only is man trying to merge with machines, but super computers are running things. In 2017, Anthony Levandowski created the Way of the Future Church, a church that worships artificial intelligence as god. He said, *"if artificial intelligence is a billion times more intelligent than humans, what else would you call it* (but God)." And on April 10, 2018 Mark Zuckerberg, CEO and co-founder of Face-book, testified before congress and said, *"in the future, AI will be controlling what Facebook deems appropriate."*

One final thing I'd like to touch on is the craze in DNA testing to determine ancestry. On the surface it is innocent and fun. But on the other hand, could it be a way to create a universal DNA database for the future antichrist? Or perhaps a way to legally harvest more DNA? Once you turn over your DNA to these companies for ancestry testing, it is legally theirs, to do with as they wish. What's to stop them from selling this DNA, your DNA, my DNA, to labs around the world for their evil purposes? I would have to say, NOTHING!

And what about this recent claim that almost everyone has some Neanderthal DNA? Where did that come from? After reading numerous articles regarding the above, I remain unconvinced. Where is the scientific evidence? What protocols were used in extracting the Neanderthal DNA? How was the Neanderthal toe preserved? What precautions were taken to prevent human contamination of the specimen? And what proof is there that no contamination occurred? How was it processed? And what protocols were followed during the processing?

Like I said, I remain unconvinced. And it doesn't help that Svante Paabo, Swedish evolutionary geneticist and Director of Max Planck Institute, revealed that when his Institute for Evolutionary Anthropology sequenced the Neanderthal genome in 2008, "Contamination was indeed an issue." It was discovered that "11% of their sample was modern human DNA." The institute claims they have beefed up their protocols and names a few of them. But was it enough?[253] Not one article I've read contained any real scientific evidence or answered the question of ongoing contamination, proper protocols, etcetera.

But some of the writers of these articles did go into great lengths discussing how their Neanderthal DNA made them moody or determined when they slept. *Really*? Based on what? Since when did supposition, conjecture or wishful thinking become science? I do know this: the scientific community can be incredibly dishonest and is notorious for protecting their pet theories. How better to protect the theory of evolution than by suddenly discovering that most of us have some Neanderthal DNA? Of course, the implication of their discovery is that we have been around for hundreds of thousands of years. Sorry, Adam and Eve came on the scene about six thousand years ago. And they were very intelligent. Adam named all the animals and then he and his offspring built sophisticated civilizations.

I like the way Gary Stearman says it. *"Darwinism presents an upward evolution, the Bible portrays a downward devolution. Darwinism paints the picture of a self-improving humanity, while the Bible teaches just the opposite, that since Adam's fall, mankind has been in the process of degeneration."*[254]

As a Christian I believe in the infallible Word of God. Romans 3:4 says, *"Let God be true, but every man a liar."* I choose to believe Him, not those trying to make a name for themselves or trying to protect their turf by coming up with flimsy, non-corroborating evidence.

And speaking of Scripture, in Daniel 2:42-43 there is an unusual verse describing Nebuchadnezzar's statue and the ten toes. It says, *"And as the toes of the feet were part of iron, and part of clay, so the kingdom shall be partly strong, and partly broken. And whereas thou sawest iron mixed with miry clay, they shall mingle themselves with the seed of men: but they shall not cleave one to another, even as iron is not mixed with clay."*

This Scripture is relevant to our subject. We know the ten toes represent the final kingdom, the revived Roman Empire. Obviously, it will not be as strong as the original Roman Empire. But it also reveals something else. In this revived empire someone or something, in other words, the "they" in Daniel, will mingle themselves with the seed of men and not cleave one to another.

Checking out some of these words in *Strong's Exhaustive Concordance* gives us better insight. First, that word "mingle" is *arab* in Hebrew and means to "commingle, mix to braid, to traffic as if by barter, become surety, a pledge, a guarantee, a kind of exchange, occupy." And that word "seed" means a physical seed. Cleave is *debeq* and/or *dabaq* and means "to cleave or cling to." It's the same word used in Genesis 2:24, *"Therefore shall a man leave his father and his mother, and shall **cleave** unto his wife: and they shall be one flesh"* It implies a sexual union. The Scripture in Daniel indicates there will be no such union.

172

So, who are "they" of the ten toes of this last kingdom? Are they hybrid men whose seed has been corrupted by fallen angels but this time not by marrying or "cleaving" to wives, but by DNA manipulation? Will this "commingling" be the result of a satanic bargain by which these rulers give up their status as true "men" for the pledge, the guarantee of global dominance and the power to rule the world? In other words, are they humans 2.0?

Remember, there are already those in the Illuminati, the Luciferin elite, who claim to be descendants of the Nephilim. At any rate, whoever "they" are, the mix is not a good one. It is weak because this kingdom will be "partly strong and partly broken." Again, we need to dig into some of the words. First, that word "strong" is *taqqip* and means "overpower." Broken is *tebar* and means "break in pieces, **judgmental punitive activity**." Partly (*qesat* and/or *qasa*) means "end, the last of a thing, cut off."

This word study suggests that because both entities are only "partly" it means their end; they are the last of a thing and will be cut off. It also implies that the partly strong will overpower the other which will break in pieces as a punitive judgment against this kingdom. But whatever it is, it will not last but be destroyed by Jesus when He returns. PRAISE GOD!

Also, in Revelation, when Jesus returns, both the antichrist and false prophet are immediately thrown into the Lake of Fire and not judged at the Great White Throne Judgment. Why is that significant? Because every human whose name is not written in the Lamb's Book of Life merits a trial before the Great White Throne. Because the antichrist and false prophet are not afforded this trial indicates they were not completely human but "other."

It's also interesting to note that some Bible scholars believe that the mark of the beast will be a computer chip implant not only able to store data and track us but that changes the DNA of man and that's why there is no forgiveness or possibility of salvation once a person takes it. If they are no longer human but "other" then that explains such a harsh judgment. Isaiah 26:13-14 talks about how the "deceased," which in Hebrew is *rephaim* here and refers to the Rephaim, will never be resurrected but will perish eternally, illustrating that non-humans or hybrids will experience the same fate.

Something to consider.

And finally, Revelation 11:18 talks about how God will destroy those who destroy the earth; those who destroy His creation like what the Nephilim did, and what the transhumanists and many scientists are doing now. And ironically, the elites will again get their wish regarding depopulating the earth because after God opens the seven seals during the first half of the Tribulation more than 1.6 billion people are going to die. What is that old saying? *Be careful what you wish for!*

Unmasking ET

What must Satan think as he surveys the condition of the earth in anticipation of implementing the final phase of his plan? Does he think it was becoming too easy? Hardly a challenge? Possibly. But surely he is pleased. Technology had captivated the world. Many of the younger, "enlightened" generations have already rejected the Most High and made themselves gods. These self-absorbed ones were open to DNA enhancement. And becoming a "superhero" suited their world view.

Still, there were holdouts, those who continued to cling to the hope that something or someone bigger than themselves was out there looking after them. Time for their hope to be realized, and in the process, scoop up those belonging to the Most High who could be fooled. The sky had been full of his handiwork for centuries. Now, it was time to up the ante.

Yes, flying machines have been around forever. As mentioned in the first chapter, these machines are described in ancient texts such as the Mahabharata, Rigweda, Ramayana, Samarangana Sutradhara and Yajurveda. They were also mentioned in the Law of the Babylonians.[255] In addition, the Egyptian Metternich Stela as well as ancient artwork in caves, on sides of mountains and elsewhere depict these machines. And the *Drona Parva*, an ancient Sanskrit text, describes midair battles between gods in flying machines.[256] Throughout history these types of things have been recorded. Indeed, in ancient times they were called "fiery chariots," "flying shields" or flying globes." And from that time to this, people have periodically seen these crafts, commonly called UFOs. No longer politically correct, UFOs are now called UAPs (Unidentified Ariel Phenomenon) by our government. But no matter what you call them, they are satanic interdimensional phenomenons, as we shall see.

It's no secret that Nazi Germany was way ahead of us in many of their sciences such as mind control and chemical weaponry. But they were especially advanced in rocketry and jet propulsion. Near the end of WWII their first jet was already rolling down the runway. If the war had lasted much longer, they would have achieved massive air superiority.

U.S. documents reveal that as far back as 1947, "The U.S. military gained information about UFO anti-gravity technology." And that this "technology came from a Nazi flying saucer program headed by a SS official named Hans Kammier, who was also connected to Hitler's V2 rocket program."[257] It appears that Hans Kammier traded this information for his freedom. It explains why the U.S. and other countries were so desperate to get their hands on these Nazi scientists and their occult knowledge.

We can assume that many of the UFO sightings are simply the result of a continuation of the Nazi flying saucer program. But not all. Remember, fallen angels used this technology eons ago. And are still using it. And how well this fits into Satan's agenda! An agenda governments around the world are currently aiding and abetting by disclosing their UFO files.

Why are they doing it?

To understand this, we need to go back a bit. By 1976, Francis Crick, co-discoverer of DNA and Nobel Laureate had concluded that human DNA was too complex to have come together by chance. Because of this, he believed our planet must have been "seeded" by aliens.

But even in the face of Crick's discovery, many scientists refused to abandon the theory of evolution. However, that changed when mapping of the human genome began in 1990 and it was discovered to be made up of 3.1 billion DNA pairs and had twenty-five thousand genes. By April 2003, the mapping was complete and made believing in Darwin's evolution difficult if not ludicrous. In response, some top scientists modified Darwin's theory by siding with Crick's theory of *panspermia,* which literally means "all seed." Neo-Darwinism is now the new accepted dogma in many scientific circles because they understand that the incredible complexity of human DNA makes it impossible to have "evolved" from any primordial ooze or soup. But not wanting to acknowledge creationism because that necessitates acknowledging a Creator, they accepted Crick's Neo-Darwinian theory of panspermia.

In the broadest sense, panspermia is the belief that our planet was seeded from outer space. There are several versions. One, that seed was carried to earth by a comet or meteor strike. Another version claims this "seeding" took place intentionally by advanced space aliens who visited earth millions of years ago and seeded it. These scientists believe that these space aliens may soon visit earth again in order to take mankind to the next level, in other words, to make us more "god-like." The latter is referred to as "direct panspermia" and was the kind championed by Dr. Crick, as well as Dr. Leslie Orgel from the Salk Institute and Richard Dawkins, former Oxford Professor and evolutionary biologist.[258]

This has exacerbated the UFO phenomenon.

Before I go further, let me say I'm not a sci-fi buff. I don't follow UFO sightings. I do not subscribe to weird science magazines and I don't believe in aliens because there are none mentioned in the Bible except for those extraterrestrial beings, the angels, both holy and fallen. And Scripture calls the fallen angels *"principalities and powers in heavenly places,"* (Ephesians 3:10, 6:12; Colossians 1:16, 2:15) meaning they not only operate on earth but in the heavens, in our atmosphere.

It is well to remember that Satan and his cohorts can masquerade as anything. And they have and continue to masquerade as aliens in UFOs. Aside from actual prototypes being created by our government, the bulk of UFO sightings are nothing more than demonic manifestations; manifestations probably also merged with technology. But this phenomenon is real and increasing. As mentioned before, many countries, including France, Great Britain, Japan, Russia, and Spain, have released their previously classified UFO files. In addition, the Vatican publicly told their faithful it was okay to believe in UFOs, and then they also released their files.

In September 2010, several major news outlets reported that the UN would make professor Mazlan Othman, a Malaysian astrophysicist, Ambassador for Extraterrestrial Contact in their Office for Outer Space Affairs, to "conduct negotiations with the first extraterrestrials that might come to this planet." Though it turned out to be untrue (Professor Othman did serve as Director for the UN Office for Outer Space Affairs in Vienna from 2007 to 2014) it shows how serious and ready the world is to accept aliens from outer space.

Perhaps there is reason. The truth is, UFO sightings, alien abductions, crop circles, animal mutilations and the like have risen sharply in recent years.

Let's look at some:

Animal mutilations—they have been going on for 40-50 years and are getting more numerous. In all that time, no arrests have been made because the police can't find any evidence: no footprints, no fingerprints, no tire tracks, no clues of any kind. There are now so many cattle and sheep mutilations that ranchers no longer report them to the authorities, and it's cutting into their profit margins. The mutilations are done with impossible precision: hearts removed without opening chest cavities, brains removed without opening skulls, etcetera. But in all cases, the blood is completely drained.

In addition, "scavengers like coyotes or vultures will not go near the carcass." And "often plant life will not grow where the carcass was dropped."[259]

Alien abductions—The number of people who claim they've been abducted by aliens has also increased drastically. But who are these abductees? Most admit they've been involved in some form of the occult. In other words, they had opened themselves up to satanic activity. The abductees claim experiments were made on them involving their sex organs: eggs removed from women, sperm from men, indicating some type of DNA harvesting. Months later, after their abduction, many of the women discovered they were pregnant. They were then re-abducted, and the fetus removed.

L.A. Marzulli, who documents these activities, believes fallen angels, in the guise of aliens, are manipulating the human genome in order to create hybrid humans to serve as shells for the habitation of demons; hybrid humans that will not be giants but will look like ordinary men and women. And all in preparation for the end times, when Satan makes his final move on planet earth. Many prophecy teachers agree with this.

The abductees are often implanted with a chip. When Dr. Roger Leir tried removing some of these chips, they migrated away from the scalpel. If the chip was damaged during removal, it could reform out of the body if submerged in the patient's blood serum. The chips were also encased with what is commonly found in the outer layer of human skin, mainly blood protein and skin cells. Dr. Leir concluded that this outer *"biological, organic, cellular substance"* was *"implant antirejection technology such as none that exists on earth today."*[260]

These chips were highly complex and technically advanced carbon nano structures. According to Wikipedia, nano technology is the manipulation of matter on an atomic and molecular level.

This subject is too vast to detail here. But those interested can get Marzulli's material where he interviews abductees, various scientists, as well as the doctor who removed these chips.

But here's the interesting thing. Some people have reported they were able to stop their abduction by invoking the name of Jesus.[261] Now, what does that tell us? If these so-called aliens were good and just interested in helping us, as some believe, why would they stop their activities when commanded to in the name of Jesus? That's exactly what a demon would do.

Demons? Really? Not so far-fetched as one might think. There are those in government research who believe that instead of extraterrestrial, these are demonic. In fact, research on this conducted from 1950 to 1970 concluded that UFOs and aliens "were supernatural entities and most likely demonic."[262] Below are more quotes:

"We are dealing with a multidimensional paraphysical phenomenon which is largely indigenous to planet Earth." Brad Steiger, *U.S. Air Force Blue Book Files*[263]

"UFO behavior is more akin to magic than physics as we know it . . . the modern UFOnauts and the demons of past days are probably identical." Dr. Pierre Guerin (scientist with French National Council for Scientific Research)[264]

"A working knowledge of occult science . . . is indispensable to UFO investigation." Trevor James[265]

In 1994, respected investigators Tommy Blann and Nelson Pacheco said the facts regarding UFOs led them to believe they were *"Satanic in origin."*[266] In 1995, former Senior Fellow Family Research Council member, Timothy J. Dailey Ph.D., agreed.

"We are witnessing a masterful satanic subterfuge that appears to involve the appearance of 'angels' and 'aliens.' Many are asking whether the coming of Antichrist can be far removed."[267]

John Mack, Pulitzer Prize-winner and Harvard psychiatrist, after studying the UFO abduction phenomenon, concluded in his *Passport to the Cosmos* that it was *"an assault of a quasi-spiritual nature."*[268] Mack researched nearly 100 cases of alien abduction and made this startling statement, *"these beings had a covert agenda to develop a hybrid race."*[269]

Respected UFO researcher and author, John Keel, believes that *"The UFO manifestations seems to be, by and large, merely minor variations of the age-old demonological phenomenon."*[270] He also concluded that, *"the UFO phenomenon was a cosmic bait-and-switch scheme perpetrated by the same entities who opposed Jesus and the disciples."*[271]

A 2003 mt.net article says it well. *"Satan and his rebel angels will not just sit by and watch God redeem the faithful, elevating mortal man to the position previously held by Satan himself and his angels. Satan's plan involves deceiving humans into accepting aliens and UFOs, and a global religion based on the occult which will pave the way for Antichrist. The main focus of this deception will be to convince humans that the Bible was wrong—that life evolved on other planets and that these alien space brothers perhaps were the ones who created humans . . . and the Bible was just a primitive misinterpretation of alien and UFO encounters."*[272]

Garry Stearman, author and T.V. host of Prophecy Watchers, adds this: *"Today, the demon and his ilk are steadily re-emerging in more and more blatant displays of strange activity. Current stories of UFO abductions, grotesque animal mutilations, genetic experiments and pseudo-technological razzle-dazzle are capped off by the furtive manifestations of the GHB, bigfoot.*

"Just beneath the surface, these phenomena are definitely connected. There is a web of activity that will produce the same sort of evil that characterized the antediluvian era. We have only to remember that ancient historians linked the demigods of old with the intrusion of Satan and his minions with the Nephilim. The fallen ones of that day seem to have been the result of dark experimentation . . . a celestial attempt to link the unseen world with our physical reality."[273]

Stearman calls the demonic entities flying these UFOs, *"trans-dimensional raiders."*

History and legend, worldwide, are full of stories of gods coming to earth then cohabitating with women and creating hybrid men. There are also numerous stories of them creating grotesque half-man-half beast creatures. And it seems like they are trying to do it again.

One of three theories are currently held by scholars regarding the origin of the mythological gods: 1) The Euhemerus View, which originated from the Greek scholar Euhemerus who believed they were deified ancient kings. 2) The Ancient Astronaut Theory, which suggests that extraterrestrials came to earth thousands of years ago and influenced our culture, religion, technology and even our human biology. More popular with movie and document-tary makers than scholars, it does encourage the theory of panspermia. But in a broader sense, it ties in well with Genesis 6:4 and the arrival of fallen angels on earth to comingle with man. And 3) The Biblical View.[274]

There is no doubt we are being programmed to accept UFOs and aliens. And one must ask, "Why?" Some in the New Age Movement believe that soon the masters of the universe, which they believe to be advanced space aliens (but really demons) will remove all those from earth whose karmas prevent the world from living in peace. And who exactly are those with "bad karmas"? First, they are the bigoted, intolerant Christians. Second, those who won't accept the elites' plan to change humanity and the world and become gods.

Perhaps this is how the world will explain the rapture when it happens, telling everyone that we, Christians, have been taken away by aliens for the good of the earth. But what awaits those who are left on earth with "bad karmas"? Those who won't bow to the elites? Well, the concentration camps that transhumanists have talked about could be a good solution. But there's always forced sterilization, forced labor camps and mental institutions. And the blueprints are already there for the elites to follow. They were created by the Nazis during the Third Reich.

Stargates and Portals:

The issue of stargates and portals needs to be addressed. Yes, according to NASA, portals or wormholes are real. In June 2012, they announced this discovery by claiming there are "hidden portals in earth's magnetic field," and "found that these portals open and close dozens of times each day."[275] A wormhole is a "fold" or shortcut between two points in space. It's often called a gate between dimensions as well as an "Einstein-Rosen bridge" because in 1935 Einstein was the first to come up with the possibility of wormholes.

A stargate, on the other hand, is the purported fiction of Roland Emmerich's 1994 film, *Stargate*. But is it really fiction? Apparently, Hindus don't think so. Their goddess of destruction, Shiva, is usually pictured dancing inside a stargate. In addition, certain Native American tribes claim they know someone who has gone through one. Hopi Indians claim to have "Star Knowledge" and talk about portals or "sky holes." They also believe that their Mythic Mountain is a portal where mythic beings land.[276]

Other Native Americans share traditions that claim they came from another star system. The Sioux believe that several portals exist in the Black Hills. In fact, "the belief in and use of stargates within the Native American culture is normal."[277] Some Blackfeet believe that Chief Mountain in Glacier National Part is a portal "between two realms."[277] The Pueblo Indians claim they often interact with entities that come through their active stargate, located in a secret place known only to them. They further claim that their medicine man oversees these meeting between the tribe and the entities. North American tribal medicine wheels, religious objects, ceremonial shields and petroglyphs all reflect their belief in portals or "sky holes."

In addition, Native American folklore is full of stories of giants and monsters. Over two hundred thousand mounds and ancient sites dot North America. They are venerated by the natives and are often the site of worship and rituals. Many giant bones have been unearthed from these mounds including a twelve-foot giant in Rancho Lompoc, California and a twelve-foot giant in West Virginia' Kanawha Valley. The grave of the former contained tools that an average man couldn't even lift. And the latter contained a skull with the familiar double rows of teeth.[278] Native American leaders call those buried in these ancient mounds, "Cloudeaters," those who descended from the sky.

There are also anomalies in Native American DNA. Many carry the mitochondrial DNA, Haplogroup T, which is also found in Egyptians and Arabs. Haplogroup T is a subgroup of Haplogroup X and found in populations once heavily infested by the Rephaim, suggesting possible ancient Nephilim influence or interaction. Haplogroup X is found in the following percentages world-wide: 2% of the Near East, Europe, and North Africa. Among Egyptians it's 14.3%, while 3% of all Native Americans carry it.[279]

What does this show? It shows not only that Native Americans have ancestral ties to Egypt but that this odd, unidentifiable DNA indicates a tampering, worldwide, of the human genome by the fallen ones during their second incursion after the flood.

Just a side note here. An April 5th, 1909 front page *Arizona Gazette* article entitled, *Explorations in Grand Canyon*, talks about two Smithsonian-funded archaeologists by the names of G.E. Kinkaid and Professor S. A. Jordan discovering ancient Egyptian artifacts in underground Grand Canyon caves. Among the supposed discoveries were weapons, copper implements, tablets engraved with hieroglyphics and mummies. In the article, Kinkaid claimed he sent a photograph he had taken as well as several relics to Washington. While Kinkaid's article was extremely detailed, it was never picked up by other news outlets and was later debunked as a hoax by the Smithsonian who said they had no record of ever hiring either Kinkaid or Jordan to explore the Grand Canyon.[280]

So, is the story true? I don't know. But the Hopi Indians, the ones who claim to have "Star Knowledge" also have a tradition that says their ancestors once lived in underground Grand Canyon caves. In addition, an old hiker's map of the Grand Canyon reveals many Egyptian names in the very area Kinkaid and Jordan claim to have made their discovery, names like Horus Temple, Osiris Temple,

Isis Temple, Tower of Set, Tower of Ra and even Shiva Temple, after the Hindu goddess. The area in question is off limits because it's deemed too "dangerous" for hikers so unfortunately no further exploration can be made. In addition, the Smithsonian has claimed these Egyptian names were given to those areas by John W. Powell (1834-1902) first director of Smithsonian's Bureau of Ethnology, with no explanation of why.

The Kinkade report could well be a giant hoax. There are many such hoaxes in archaeology. And I'm not looking to prove or disprove it. I only mention it because of the Egyptian connection. If it's true, I'm sure more information will eventually come to light.

But it shouldn't surprise us that many world cultures contain, not only in their DNA, but also their folklore, hints of the fallen ones. Many structures worldwide are purported to be portals or gateways to another dimension or world. A few of them are mentioned here: Stonehenge; the Euphrates River bottom; Gate of the Gods in Hayu Marca, Peru; Gobekli Tepe, oldest stone temple in the world; all believed to be portals. Place of the Gods in Abu Ghurab, Egypt, believed to be a stargate; Abydos, Egypt, also believed to be a stargate and features hieroglyphics of modern

Sylvia Bambola

military weapons and aircraft; Gate of the Sun in
Bolivia which depicts figures wearing space
helmets; Ranmasu Uyana Stargate in Sri Lanka
which has a star map.[281]

Many believe that what Nimrod was trying to
accomplish in his Tower of Babel was to create a
portal, a gateway to heaven, giving the fallen angels
access to earth.

It is believed that in order to access a portal, a
stargate is needed. I don't know if that's true, but I
do know many scientists today are exploring this,
especially at CERN.

The scientists' connection:

It goes without saying that many in the scientific
community are sincere and honorable and have
only good intentions. But many are not and
populate numerous disciplines across the spectrum.
I've already mentioned how Nazi scientists
poisoned the pool. Their protégés now follow in
their footsteps, claiming to be atheists or humanists
and declaring there is no God while wanting to
become gods themselves. The irony is that in the
2004 case of "James J. Kaufman vs. Gary R.
MacCaughtry" the courts ruled that secular
humanism was a religion.[282] But if it's a religion, it's

a failed one, bringing poverty and enslavement to its adherents by its inevitable lead to socialism and communism. And now these same people hope to find the "Higgs Boson" or "God particle" in order to discover the secret of creation and in so doing may bring destruction instead. Here's what SaneScience said about it in 2011.

"Nobel Prize hungry physicists are racing each other and stopping at nothing to try to find the supposed 'Higgs Boson' (aka God) Particle, among others, and are risking nothing less than the annihilation of the earth and all life in endless experiments hoping to prove a theory when urgent tangible problems face the planet.

The European Organization for Nuclear Research's (CERN) new Large Hadron Collider (LHC) is the world's most powerful atom smasher that will soon be firing groups of billions of heavy subatomic particles at each other at nearly the speed of light to create Miniature Big Bangs producing Micro Black Holes, Strangelets, Anti-Matter and other potentially cataclysmic phenomena."[283]

CERN, the European Organization for Nuclear Research, was founded in 1954. Within the logo itself is the number 666. Its lab is located near Geneva on the Franco-Swiss Border. Its initial mission was to determine if the "God Particle" or the glue that holds everything together, was real. In

July 2012, CERN claimed to have found it. But this effort was not made to prove the existence of God. Far from it. In truth, they have come to believe they are god, and wanted to find the answer to creation in order to replicate it in some way.

And what better tip off to their mindset than the statue of Shiva they placed at the entrance of their complex in 2004. It is the only religious statue or artifact on the premises. Shiva Nataraja, the Hindu goddess of destruction, is supposed to destroy the world in order to make room for a new one. Sound familiar? Isn't that what the New World Order is trying to do? Destroy what exists in order to remake the world in their image?

And Shiva does the destroy-the-world-dance in a stargate! Remember, in order to enter a portal or wormhole it's believed one must go through a stargate. And "the key to creating a wormhole is the creation of negative particles. And creating negative particles is what the CERN project is all about."[284] Does that mean CERN intends to become the stargate to the black holes they create?

And what do you know? CERN is an abbreviation for the Celtic god, Cernnunos, god of the underworld![285] This atom smasher lies deep underground and its magnets are "one hundred thousand times more powerful than the gravitational pull of earth."[286] As already stated, it produces miniature Big Bangs resulting in micro black holes, strangelets, anti-matter and other potentially harmful results. Even Stephen Hawking, in 2015, voiced his concern over what the LHC, the Large Hadron Collider, was creating.[287]

In addition, CERN is located near an ancient temple to Apollo. Another name for Apollo is Apollyon, which the Bible, in Revelation, calls the king of the hybrid creatures in the Abyss. And here's another disturbing fact: in 2016 a mock human sacrifice was conducted in front of the Shiva statue, and the video of it was put on YouTube. CERN officials said it was just some of their people having fun.[288] *Fun?* Since when is pretending to kill someone, considered fun?

Since finding the Higgs Boson, CERN's new objective became searching out "dark matter" or the heavier than normal matter they believe exists in space. However, their second stated goal was to "open a door to a different dimension." CERN's director of research, Sergio Bertolucci, said the LHC could *"create a door to an extra dimension."*[289] Read, portal and stargate! In simple language, what they're looking to do is punch a hole into another dimension. According to Geordie Rose (quantum computing advocate and founder of D-Wave) they have already done it. He also claims that not only have they broken into another dimension but that they are sending and receiving messages from that dimension.[290] Congratulations! You are now conversing with demons!

The Catholic connection:

For the first time in history a Jesuit sits on the throne of Saint Peter. Jesuits are the liberal wing of the Catholic Church. As previously mentioned, Father Malachi Martin, Catholic theologian, advisor to three Popes and official Vatican researcher of the Dead Sea Scrolls, disclosed in his 1987 book, *The Jesuits: The Society of Jesus and the Betrayal of the Roman Catholic Church,* the satanic cabal within the Jesuit community. He also disclosed the Jesuits' deep interest in all things extraterrestrial.

Beginning in the 1970s and for the next twenty years, exorcist and member of the Vatican governing body, Monsignor Carrado Balducci, promoted the idea that ET was real, was already interacting with earth and that the Vatican knew it.[291] In 1978 Jesuit George V. Coyne became director of the Vatican Observatory and began promoting the idea that "all religions led to the same God."[292]

The Jesuits now have an observatory in Mt Graham, Arizona. Mt. Graham is one of the four holiest mountains for Western Apaches and was built despite Native American objection. In essence, it's a portal, a stargate from which, according to Apaches, the "Mountain Spirits or Gaahn enter and exit a doorway." It is a place where they believe "entities" have passed through since time began.[293] Dr. Moses, the Apache nation's medicine man, when retelling the legend of his people, speaks about the story of creation, a "reptilian deceiver," cannibalistic giants and portals or stargates. This was precisely why Mt. Graham was chosen by the Vatican.

The Mt. Graham observatory has an advanced telescope call LUCIFER (short for Large Binocular Telescope Near-Infrared Utility with Camera and Integral Field Unit for Extragalactic Research). Jesuit priest, Guy Consol-magno, the Vatican's leading astronomer and one of the scientists at Mt. Graham talks about *the Jesus Seed,* postulating the theory that every planet supporting intelligent life also had a "Christ."[294] He further purposes that more moral and highly developed species than man may exist elsewhere and *may come here to evangelize us.*[295] Part of Consolmagno's speculation includes Jesus being a *Child of other races.* But it doesn't stop there. Former vice director of the Vatican Observatory Research Group on Mt. Graham, Dr.

Christopher Corbally, "believes our image of God will have to change if evidence of alien life is confirmed by scientists."[296]

The Vatican's Pontifical Academy of Sciences, in 2009, invited several astronomers, geologists, biologists, and Catholic theologians to "discuss the existence of extraterrestrials and the theological implications of disclosure."[297] The Vatican seems bent on finding life in outer space. That's because the Jesuits don't believe in intelligent design and creationism. They are actively looking for "exoplanets that are habitable."[298] In addition, they are currently studying the possibility of panspermia by asteroid, and if discovered, believe it will "inspire a global religion." Read, a one-world occult religion that removes the God of the Bible, deifies the fallen angels and sets up man to become demi-gods.

We see that the Vatican has been interested in extraterrestrials for years. Their Jesuit scientists claim they are observing UFOs daily but as yet have made no contact. These same astronomer/priests believe that once contact is made **the gospels and Christianity and the concept of salvation will need to be redefined.** They believe strongly in the possibility that Jesus was an alien, an advanced superbeing, but only one of many. What will happen to millions of sincere Catholics, who love the Lord but are not grounded in God's Word, when the Catholic Church finally comes out with this "alien gospel"?

I believe there will be a massive falling away.

These Catholics, feeling allegiance to the Pope, will be deceived when their pontiff declares that we were seeded by superior beings from outer space and that Jesus was merely one of them. It's heartbreaking and illustrates the importance of knowing what the Bible says, so if our church or denomination begins preaching error, we will recognize it. Churches are fallible, but God's Word remains solid. It is well to remember that Jesus is the One who saves us, not any church.

We are being set up for an "alien gospel."

It's a gospel that proclaims "aliens" (demons) landed on earth and were the progenitors of mankind; that humanity was the product of extraterrestrial origin; and that they will come back to "save" the earth. In addition, we can all become "gods" if we mingle our seed with technology (machines) or animals or plants in order to increase our lifespan, our hearing, our sight, our mental powers, etcetera.

This concept is already going mainstream. Movies like *Avatar, Edge of Tomorrow, X-Men, When Aliens Come . . .What Do They Want?* and TV series like the *X Files* are programming us. And movies about superheroes are the big rage. Through them we become familiar with and even accept and come to like aliens such as Superman or DNA altered humans such as Spiderman and even demonic pagan idols like Thor, a hammer-wielding super-being who was probably based on a Nephilim.

While these movies are entertaining, they also produce a dangerous side effect, a subtle condition-ing of the mind to accept as good or even desirable, the concept of being something "other" than human. Then, when demonic science puts forth the means for millions, if not billions, to enhance themselves, the question in people's minds, especially the young, will be, "Why would anyone want to be a 'puny' human when they can be enhanced and become a 'superhero'?" We now have a generation who has never known anything but technology. They are comfortable with it, see it as good, perhaps even indispensable. And I fear too many will see nothing wrong with giving up their humanity in order to achieve "superpowers."

Conclusion:

So, what is the coming deception? Just more of the same? That slugs crawled out of the primordial soup and evolved into man after millions of years? No. It's that our planet was seeded by aliens. That our lineage is from aliens, from superbeings who are still looking out for us. And Jesus was such a super-being, but only one of many. That the Bible is an outdated book full of ignorance and primitive, inaccurate stories that try, incorrectly, to explain how things really are. In addition, these superbeings will return in order to bring mankind to the next level of evolution, which transhumanists call the "fifth epoch" and is akin to godhood. But this can only be achieved by having the proper "karma" and through advanced genetic manipulation, meaning by the mingling of our DNA with things like machines or animals or plants and becoming "other." And that people who don't conform are dangerous and a blot on society and need to be dealt with either by extermination or enslavement.

This is the goal of the New World Order. This is what the *New Atlantis* will look like. This is what the secret societies, the transhumanists and other scientists, the elites, the Illuminati are trying to bring about. The very ceremonies performed by groups such as the Freemasons center around the return of Nimrod (Osiris) resurrecting through a portal to complete his unfinished work symbolized by the missing top cap of the pyramid on the back of the U.S. dollar. And when he does, he will usher in this *New Atlantis*, this New World Order, a Utopia on earth, and all without God.

It's the same lie that Satan told Eve, and the same tactics employed by the fallen angels who cohabitated with women to corrupt mankind and produced monstrosities. It's a lie that is being promoted everywhere you care to look. And it's a lie that many are beginning to believe. It's a lie that seeks to discredit the need for salvation or God. It aims at the very heart of who Jesus is and what the Word says, and instead, promotes a world where we become "god."

And why does Satan want us to become "gods"? Because there are only three kingdoms. I list them in order of power: God's Kingdom, Satan's Kingdom and Kingdom of Self. If God is not king over us and we are our own god, our own king, then God's protection will not cover us. We will be left wide open for Satan's attacks because the Kingdom of Self is the only kingdom Satan can conquer.

But praise the God of Heaven, it will not end there. Hebrews 9:23 speaks about the necessity for purging the heavens, an obvious reference to the sin of Satan and his cohorts. And Isaiah 24:21 talks about two punishments that will occur in the last days; the punishment of the "host of the high ones that are on high" and the "kings of the earth." There is a day of judgment coming. This is when all accounts will be settled, both heavenly ones and earthly ones. And Scripture tells us there will be no resurrection for the Nephilim or Rephaim (Isaiah 26:14, 26:19).

It's easy for Christians to believe that Jesus' death was all about us. And it was. But it was about so much more. It was about redeeming all of creation which groans, and about putting an end to the cosmic battle that has been raging for millennia.

In the end, God wins and so do we.

*"And the kingdom and dominion, and the greatness of the kingdom under the whole heaven, shall be given to the people of the saints of the most High, whose kingdom is an **everlasting** kingdom, and all dominions shall serve and obey him."* Daniel 7:27

Amen! Praise God!

Author's Note

So, what should Christians do now?" Hide in caves or stop living our lives? Absolutely not! We don't know God's timing. The end could still be a distant tomorrow because God is long-suffering and forbearing and He desires that everyone come into the saving knowledge of Jesus. What we need to do is live our lives all out for God. Be the best student, housewife, mother, father, doctor, businessman or businesswoman or whatever our assignment is, and "do it all unto the Lord."

We live in exciting times, times when God wants to show Himself strong through His church, which means you and me. And that means you and I need to be lights in this dark world and live by the Word of God. We also need to stand up and be counted by exhibiting His love, mercy and power as we go through our lives touching those people who are within our sphere of influence.

But we also need to understand that we are in a fierce battle and Satan, like a roaring lion, is going about seeking those who he may devour. Because of this, we need to know who we are in Christ as well as exercise our God-given authority over him.

In this world everything is uncertain except for God's love and the fact that He has provided a way for us to be with Him for all eternity. If you don't know Him, this is a good time to ask Him to come into your life. Pray: Dear Jesus, I know I am a sinner and cannot save myself. I acknowledge that You are the Savior, that You died on the cross to save me from my sins and I accept what you did for me. I ask You to come into my heart, to be my Savior and Lord and I will live for You all the rest of my days. And I pray all of this in Jesus' name, amen.

God is gracious. If you meant it, He has heard.

Love and blessings to all,
Sylvia Bambola
sylviabambola45@gmail.com

Notes

1. Stephen Quayle & Dr. Thomas R. Horn, *Unearthing the Lost World of the Cloudeaters* (Crane, MO: Defender, 2017), 12-13, 24-25; "Sumerian King List," https://en.wikipedia.org/wiki/Sumerian_King_List.
2. Ibid., 16.
3. Sais, Egypt, https://en.wikipedia.org/wiki/Sais,_Egypt.
4. Stephen Quayle, *Genesis 6 Giants, Master Builders of Prehistoric and Ancient Civilizations* (Bozeman, MT: End Time Thunder Publishers, 2010), 100-101.
5. Shangri-La https://en.wikipedia.org/wiki/Shangri-La.
6. Avalon, https://en.wikipedia.org/wiki/Avalon.
7. Buyan, https://www.definitions.net/definition/Buyan.
8. Kitezh, http://kitezh.com/kitezh.htm.

9. Datta, Amaresh (1 January 2006) *The Encyclopedia of Indian Literature* (Volume Two)

10. Stephen Quayle & Dr. Thomas R. Horn, *Unearthing the Lost World of the Cloudeaters* (Crane, MO: Defender, 2017), 91.

11. Ibid., 92.

12. Rigveda, https://www.britannica.com/topic/Rigveda.

13. Stephen Quayle & Dr. Thomas R. Horn, *Unearthing the Lost World of the Cloudeaters* (Crane, MO: Defender, 2017), 91.

14. "What Powered the Vimana, the 6,000-year-old Flying Machines of Ancient India?" Ancient Code Online, http://www.ancient-code.com/powered-vimana-6000-year-old-flying-machines-ancient-india/, (May 2016).

15. Antikythera mechanism, https://en.wikipedia.org/wiki/Antikythera_mechanism.

16. Paul McGuire & Troy Anderson, *The Babylon Code* (NY, NY, *Faith Words*, Hachette Book Group, 2015), 189.

17. Stephen Quayle, *Genesis 6 Giants, Master Builders of Prehistoric and Ancient Civilizations* (Bozeman, MT: End Time Thunder Publishers, 2010), 86.

18. Stephen Quayle, *Terminated* (Bozeman, MT: End Time Thunder Publishers, 2018), 145.

19. Baalbek,
https://en.wikipedia.org/wiki/Baalbek.
20. Stephen Quayle & Dr. Thomas R. Horn,
Unearthing the Lost World of the Cloudeaters
(Crane, MO: Defender, 2017), 78.
21. Mars, https://mars.nasa.gov/mars-exploration/missions/mars-global-surveyor/.
22. Stephen Quayle & Dr. Thomas R. Horn,
Unearthing the Lost World of the Cloudeaters
(Crane, MO: Defender, 2017), 78.
23. Cris Putnam & Thomas Horn, *Exo-Vaticana*
(Crane, MO: Defender, 2013), 477.
24. Ibid., 475.
25. Stephen Quayle & Dr. Thomas R. Horn,
Unearthing the Lost World of the Cloudeaters
(Crane, MO: Defender, 2017), 125.
26. Stephen Quayle, *Angel Wars* (Bozeman, MT:
End Time Thunder Publishers, 2011), 11-12.
27. Stephen Quayle & Dr. Thomas R. Horn,
Unearthing the Lost World of the Cloudeaters
(Crane, MO: Defender, 2017), 87.
28. Ibid., 97.
29. Ibid., 125.
30. Ibid., 82.
31. R. Laird Harris, Gleason L. Archer, Jr., Bruce
K. Waltke, *Theological Wordbook of the Old
Testament* (Chicago, IL: Moody Publishers,
1980), 252.

32. *The New Complete Works of JOSEPHUS*, Translated by William Whiston, Commentary by Paul L. Maier (Grand Rapids, MI: Kregel Publications, 1999), *Flavius Josephus, Antiquities of the Jews – Book I*, chapter 3:1

33. Ryan Pitterson, *Judgment of the Nephilim* (NY, NY: Days of Noe Publishing, 2017), 142.

34. Ibid.

35. Ibid., 142-143.

36. Steve Schmutzer, *"Who are the Sons of God in Genesis 6: The Prophecy Watcher,* December 2018, p. 28.

37. Saint Augustine, "Concerning the long life of men before the flood, and the greater size of their bodies." Chapter XI, pp. 322-325.

38. Ryan Pitterson, *Judgment of the Nephilim* (NY, NY: Days of Noe Publishing, 2017), 145.

39. *The Researchers Library of Ancient Texts* Volume 1, Jasher 4:18 (Crane, MO: Defender).

40. Dr. Michael Lake, *The Shinar Directive* (Crane, MO: Defender, 2014), 50-51.

41. Stephen Quayle, *Angel Wars* (Bozeman, MT: End Time Thunder Publishers, 2011), 111.

42. Paul McGuire & Troy Anderson, *The Babylon Code* (NY, NY: *Faith Words,* Hachette Book Group, 2015), 177.

43. Stephen Quayle, *Genesis 6 Giants, Master Builders of Prehistoric and Ancient Civilizations* (Bozeman, MT: End Time Thunder Publishers, 2010), 59.

44. Ken Johnson, Th.D., *Ancient Book of Enoch*, Copyright 2012, by Ken Johnson, Th.D., pp. 5-7.

45. Ibid., 1 Enoch 1:9.

46. Book of Enoch, https://wn.wikipedia.org/wiki/BookofEnoch.

47. Ken Johnson, Th.D., *Ancient Book of Enoch*, Copyright 2012, by Ken Johnson, Th.D. I Enoch pp. 14-15.

48. Ibid., 1 Enoch 6:1-8.

49. Stephen Quayle, *Angel Wars* (Bozeman, MT: End Time Thunder Publishers, 2011), 337.

50. Stephen Quayle & Dr. Thomas R. Horn, *Unearthing the Lost World of the Cloudeaters* (Crane, MO: Defender, 2017), 395.

51. Ken Johnson, Th.D., *Ancient Book of Enoch*, Copyright 2012, by Ken Johnson, Th.D., 1 Enoch 7:1-6.

52. *The Researchers Library of Ancient Texts* Volume 1, *Jasher* (Crane, MO: Defender), Jasher 4:18.

53. Stephen Quayle, *Angel Wars* (Bozeman, MT: End Time Thunder Publishers, 2011), 46.

54. Ken Johnson, Th.D., *Ancient Book of Enoch*, Copyright 2012, by Ken Johnson, Th.D., 1 Enoch 8:1-2.

55. Ibid., 1 Enoch 10:6.

56. Stephen Quayle, *Angel Wars* (Bozeman, MT: End Time Thunder Publishers, 2011), 51; Otzi, https://en.wikipedia.org/wiki/otzi.

57. Ken Johnson, Th.D., *Ancient Book of Enoch*, Copyright 2012, by Ken Johnson, Th.D., 1 Enoch 12:5-6.

58. Ibid., 1 Enoch 9:1-11.

59. Ibid., pp. 20-21.

60. Stephen Quayle, *Angel Wars* (Bozeman, MT: End Time Thunder Publishers, 2011), 27.

61. *The Zondervan Pictorial Encyclopedia of the Bible*, Volume 2, page 727 (Grand Rapids, Michigan: Regency Reference Library, 1976).

62. Bodie Hodge, *Tower of Babel, The Cultural History of Our Ancestors* (Green Forest, AR: Master Books, division of the New Leaf Publishing Group, Inc., 2013), 73.

63. Ibid., 124.

64. Berossus, https://www.livius.org/articles/misc/great-flood/flood3 t-berossus/.

65. Dr. Michael Lake, *The Shinar Directive* (Crane, MO: Defender, 2014), 165.

66. Stephen Quayle, *Angel Wars* (Bozeman, MT: End Time Thunder Publishers, 2011), 117.

67. George H. Pember, *Earth's Earliest Ages* (Crane, MO: Defense Publishing, 2012), 174.

68. Stephen Quayle, *Angel Wars* (Bozeman, MT, End Time Thunder Publishers, 2011) 88.

69. Paul McGuire & Troy Anderson, *The Babylon Code* (NY, NY: *Faith Words*, Hachette Book Group, 2015), 39.

70. Dr. Michael Lake, *The Shinar Directive* (Crane, MO: Defender, 2014), 79.

71. *Pandemonium's Engine*, Dr. J. Michael Bennett, Ph.D., "Nimrod: The First and Future Transhuman 'Super Soldier,'" p. 91, (Crane, MO: Defender, 2011); Bodie Hodge, *Tower of Babel, The Cultural History of Our Ancestors* (Green Forest, AR: Master Books, division of the New Leaf Publishing Group, Inc., 2013), 214; Stephen Quayle & Dr. Thomas R. Horn, *Unearthing the Lost World of the Cloudeaters* (Crane, MO: Defender, 2017), 174.

72. Stephen Quayle, *Angel Wars* (Bozeman, MT: End Time Thunder Publishers, 2011), 115-116.

73. Paul McGuire & Troy Anderson, *The Babylon Code* (NY, NY: *Faith Words*, Hachette Book Group, 2015), 44.

74. George H. Pember, *Earth's Earliest Ages* (Crane, MO: Defense Publishing, 2012), 109.

75. Thomas Horn & Cris Putnam, *Petrus Romanus* (Crane, MO: Defender, 2012), 122.

76. Stephen Quayle, *Angel Wars* (Bozeman, MT: End Time Thunder Publishers, 2011), 93.

77. Stephen Quayle, *Genesis 6 Giants, Master Builders of Prehistoric and Ancient Civilizations* (Bozeman, MT: End Time Thunder Publishers, 2010), 467.

78. Stephen Quayle, *Angel Wars* (Bozeman, MT: End Time Thunder Publishers, 2011), 76.

79. Ken Johnson, Th.D., *Ancient Testaments of the Patriarchs, Autobiographies from the Dead Sea Scrolls*, Copyright 2017 by Ken Johnson, Th.D., p. 105.

80. Stephen Quayle & Dr. Thomas R. Horn, *Unearthing the Lost World of the Cloudeaters* (Crane, MO: Defender, 2017), 338-339.

81. Stephen Quayle, *Genesis 6 Giants, Master Builders of Prehistoric and Ancient Civilizations* (Bozeman, MT: End Time Thunder Publishers, 2010), 256.

82. Ibid.

83. Ibid.

84. Ibid., 193.

85. Ibid., 260.

86. Ibid., 258.

87. Ibid., 193.

88. Stephen Quayle, *Angel Wars* (Bozeman, MT: End Time Thunder Publishers, 2011), 133.

89. Stephen Quayle & Dr. Thomas R. Horn, *Unearthing the Lost World of the Cloudeaters* (Crane, MO: Defender, 2017), 319.

90. Ibid., 279-283.

91. Ibid., 308-318.

92. Roanoke Colony, https://en.wikipedia.org/wiki/Roanoke_Colony.

93. Popham Colony, https://en.wikipedia.org/wiki/Popham_Colony.

94. Jamestown, https://www.nps.gov/jame/learn/historyculture/a-short-history-of-jamestown.htm.

95. Thomas Horn, *Apollyon Rising 2012* (Crane, MO: Defender, 2009), 71.

96. Paul McGuire & Troy Anderson, *The Babylon Code* (NY, NY: *Faith Words*, Hachette Book Group, 2015), 205.

97. "The Mastery of Life" http://www.rosicrucian.org/about/master/master.pdf pg. 31.

98. Thomas Horn, *Apollyon Rising 2012* (Crane, MO: Defender, 2009), 324.

99. Plymouth Colony, https://en.wikipedia.org/wiki/Pilgrims_(Plymouth_Colony).

100. John Winthrop, https://worldhistoryproject.org/1630/john-

winthrop-delivers-city-upon-a-hill-sermon-aboard-the-arbella-heading-en-route-to-colonial-america.

101.   Philbrick, Nathaniel. *Mayflower: A Story of Courage, Community, and War*, (New York, NY: Viking, 2006).

102.   Mayflower Compact, https://en.wikipedia.org/wiki/Mayflower_Compact.

103.   Thomas Horn, *Apollyon Rising 2012* (Crane, MO: Defender, 2009), 16-17.

104.   Dr. Stanley Monteith, *Brotherhood of Darkness* (Oklahoma City, OK: Hearthstone Publishing, 2000), 74.

105.   Ibid., 120-121.

106.   Dr. Michael Lake, *The Shinar Directive* (Crane, MO: Defender, 2014), 194.

107.   Dr. Stanley Monteith, *Brotherhood of Darkness* (Oklahoma City, OK: Hearthstone Publishing, 2000), 120.

108.   Thomas Horn, *Apollyon Rising 2012* (Crane, MO: Defender, 2009), 19.

109.   Warren Weston, *Father of Lies* (London: cir. 1930), 29.

110.   Stephen Quayle, *Angel Wars* (Bozeman, MT: End Time Thunder Publishers, 2011), 221.

111. Manly P. Hall, *The Secret Destiny of America*, (The Philosophical Research Society, Inc., Los Angeles, CA, 1944), 126.

112. Dr. Stanley Monteith, *Brotherhood of Darkness* (Oklahoma City, OK: Hearthstone Publishing, 2000), 73.

113. Thomas Horn, *Apollyon Rising 2012* (Crane, MO: Defender, 2009), 110.

114. Ibid., 123.

115. Thomas Horn & Cris Putnam, *Petrus Romanus* (Crane, MO: Defender, 2012), 140.

116. Ibid., 130.

117. *Pandemonium's Engine*, J. Michael Bennett, Ph.D., Nimrod: "The First and Future Transhuman 'Super Soldier,'" p. 98, (Crane, MO: Defender, 2011).

118. Paul McGuire & Troy Anderson, *The Babylon Code* (NY, NY: *Faith Words*, Hachette Book Group, 2015), 13.

119. Thomas Horn, *Apollyon Rising 2012* (Crane, MO: Defender, 2009), 138.

120. Paul McGuire & Troy Anderson, *The Babylon Code* (NY, NY: *Faith Words*, Hachette Book Group, 2015), 40.

121. Dr. Michael Lake, *The Shinar Directive* (Crane, MO: Defender, 2014), 239.

122. Dr. Stanley Monteith, *Brotherhood of Darkness* (Oklahoma City, OK: Hearthstone Publishing, 2000), 18-36.

123.   Cris Putnam & Thomas Horn, *Exo-Vaticana* (Crane, MO: Defender, 2013), 211.

124.   Dr. Stanley Monteith, *Brotherhood of Darkness* (Oklahoma City, OK: Hearthstone Publishing, 2000), p. 71; p. 99.

125.   Ibid., p. 29; p. 33.

126.   Paul McGuire & Troy Anderson, *The Babylon Code* (NY, NY: *Faith Words*, Hachette Book Group, 2015), 55.

127.   Ibid., 170.

128.   Ibid.

129.   *Pandemonium's Engine*, J. Michael Bennett, Ph.D., "Nimrod: The First and Future Transhuman 'Super Soldier,'" p. 97 (Crane, MO: Defender, 2011).

130.   Dr. Stanley Monteith, *Brotherhood of Darkness* (Oklahoma City, OK: Hearthstone Publishing, 2000), 49-51.

131.   Dr. Michael Lake, *The Shinar Directive* (Crane, MO: Defender, 2014), 113.

132.   Dr. Stanley Monteith, *Brotherhood of Darkness* (Oklahoma City, OK: Hearthstone Publishing, 2000), 56.

133.   Dr. Michael Lake, *The Shinar Directive* (Crane, MO: Defender, 2014), 184-185.

134.   Thomas Horn, *Apollyon Rising 2012* (Crane, MO: Defender, 2009), 47-48.

135.   Dr. Stanley Monteith, *Brotherhood of Darkness* (Oklahoma City, OK: Hearthstone Publishing, 2000), 73-74.

136.   Ibid., p. 36.

137.   Dr. Michael Lake, *The Shinar Directive* (Crane, MO: Defender, 2014), 207.

138.   Dr. Stanley Monteith, *Brotherhood of Darkness* (Oklahoma City, OK: Hearthstone Publishing, 2000), 129.

139.   United Nations, "The Millennium Development Goals Report, 2012," p. 67.

140.   Dr. Stanley Monteith, *Brotherhood of Darkness* (Oklahoma City, OK: Hearthstone Publishing, 2000), 39.

141.   Paul McGuire & Troy Anderson, *The Babylon Code* (NY, NY: *Faith Words*, Hachette Book Group, 2015), 81.

142.   Dr. Stanley Monteith, *Brotherhood of Darkness* (Oklahoma City, OK: Hearthstone Publishing, 2000), 42.

143.   Ibid., p. 40.

144.   Dr. Michael Lake, *The Shinar Directive* (Crane, MO: Defender, 2014), 239.

145.   Thomas Horn, *Apollyon Rising 2012* (Crane, MO: Defender, 2009), 51.

146.   Billy Crone, "Apostasy of the Church," *Prophecy in the News Magazine,* March 2015, pp. 11-14.

147.　　　Carl Teichrib, "Report from the Toronto Parliament of the World's Religions," *Prophecy Watcher Magazine,* June 2019, pp. 26-37.

148.　　　Dr. Michael Lake, *The Shinar Directive* (Crane, MO: Defender, 2014), 335-336.

149.　　　Ibid., p. 340.

150.　　　Thomas Horn & Cris Putnam, *Petrus Romanus* (Crane, MO: Defender, 2012), 449.

151.　　　Cris Putnam & Thomas Horn, *Exo-Vaticana* (Crane, MO: Defender, 2013), 533.

152.　　　Ibid., p. 535.

153.　　　Thomas Horn, *Apollyon Rising 2012* (Crane, MO: Defender, 2009), 328.

154.　　　Cris Putnam & Thomas Horn, *Exo-Vaticana* (Crane, MO: Defender, 2013), 533.

155.　　　https://www.catholicculture.org/news/headlines/index.cfm?storyid=20454.

156.　　　Thomas Horn & Cris Putnam, *Petrus Romanus* (Crane, MO: Defender, 2012), 238.

157.　　　Ibid., p. 91.

158.　　　Ibid., pp. 90-93.

159.　　　Ibid., p. 51.

160.　　　Ibid., p. 90.

161.　　　Ibid., p. 91.

162.　　　Ibid., p. 244.

163.　　　Cris Putnam & Thomas Horn, *Exo-Vaticana* (Crane, MO: Defender, 2013), 307-308.

164.   Ibid., p. 38.

165.   Thomas Horn & Cris Putnam, *Petrus Romanus* (Crane, MO: Defender, 2012), 466.

166.   https://www.thedailybeast.com/does-pope-francis-believe-christians-and-muslims-worship-the-same-god.

167.   Anthony Faiola, "8 of Pope Francis's most liberal statements," *The Washington Post*, September 7, 2015.

168.   John-Henry Westen, *LifeSiteNews*, October 2013.

169.   John-Henry Westen, *LifeSiteNews*, March 2015.

170.   John-Henry Westen, *LifeSiteNews*, February 2016.

171.   Cris Putnam & Thomas Horn, *Exo-Vaticana* (Crane, MO: Defender, 2013), 211-212; Thomas Horn & Cris Putnam, *Petrus Romanus* (Crane, MO: Defender, 2012), 471.

172.   Caitlyn Kennedy, "Why did Earth's surface temperature stop rising in the past decade?" September 1. 2018, p. 1, http://www.climate.gov/.

173.   Stephen Quayle, *Angel Wars* (Bozeman, MT: End Time Thunder Publishers, 2011), 297.

174.   Ibid.

175.   Ibid.

176.　　Ronald Bailey, *Eco Scam, The False Prophets of Ecological Apocalypse* (NY, NY: St. Martin's Press, 1993), 15.

177.　　Ibid., pp. 64-65.

178.　　Peter Rogers, "Climate Change and Global Warming," *Environmental Science and Technology* 24:4 (1990), 429.

179.　　Alexander King and Bertrand Schneider, *The First Global Revolution: A Report by the Council of the Club of Rome* (New York: Pantheon, 1991), 127.

180.　　Ronald Bailey, *Eco Scam, The False Prophets of Ecological Apocalypse* (NY, NY: St. Martin's Press, 1993), 77.

181.　　https://climateandsecurity.org/2015/07/08/un-security-council-meeting-on-climate-change-as-a-threat-multiplier-for-global-security/.

182.　　Ronald Bailey, *Eco Scam, The False Prophets of Ecological Apocalypse* (NY, NY: St. Martin's Press, 1993), 84.

183.　　"Another Ice Age?" *Time Magazine*, June 24, 1974.

184.　　Nigel Calder, "In the Grip of a New Ice Age?" *International Wildlife* (June 1975), 33-35.

185.　　Ronald Bailey, *Eco Scam, The False Prophets of Ecological Apocalypse* (NY, NY: St. Martin's Press, 1993), 84.

186. Ibid., p. 43.
187. Ibid., p. 47.
188. Bjorn Lomborg, *The Skeptical Environmentalist, Measuring the Real State of the World* (Cambridge, UK: Cambridge University Press, 2001), 273.
189. Ronald Bailey, *Eco Scam, The False Prophets of Ecological Apocalypse* (NY, NY: St. Martin's Press, 1993), 132.
190. Ibid., p. 119-120.
191. Bjorn Lomborg, *The Skeptical Environmentalist, Measuring the Real State of the World* (Cambridge, UK: Cambridge University Press, 2001), 13.
192. Ron Arnold, *Undue Influence* (Bellevue, Washington: The Free Enterprise Press, Distributed by Merril Press, 1999), 14.
193. Ibid., p. 16.
194. Ibid., p. 20.
195. Archie Ruprecht, "Ask Not for Whom the Owl Hoots," Letter to the editor, *The New York Times* (March 14, 1992), 24.
196. Ronald Bailey, *Eco Scam, The False Prophets of Ecological Apocalypse* (NY, NY: St. Martin's Press, 1993), 7.
197. Ron Arnold, *Ecoterror, The Violent Agenda To Save Nature* (Bellevue, Washington: The Free Enterprise Press, Distributed by Merril Press, 1997), 225.

198.   Ibid.
199.   Ibid., p. 11.
200.   Ronald Bailey, *Eco Scam, The False Prophets of Ecological Apocalypse* (NY, NY: St. Martin's Press, 1993), 8.
201.   Ibid.
202.   Ibid., p. 1.
203.   Ibid., p. 16.
204.   Ibid., p. 22.
205.   Ibid., pp. 5-6.
206.   Ibid., p. 11.
207.   Bjorn Lomborg, *The Skeptical Environmentalist, Measuring the Real State of the World* (Cambridge, UK: Cambridge University Press, 2001), 303; 317.
208.   Ibid., p. 309.
209.   Ronald Bailey, *Eco Scam, The False Prophets of Ecological Apocalypse* (NY, NY: St. Martin's Press, 1993), 145.
210.   Ibid., p. 156.
211.   Ibid., p. 165.
212.   Ibid., p. 167.
213.   Dr. Michael Lake, *The Shinar Directive* (Crane, MO: Defender, 2014), 64.
214.   Stephen Quayle, *Angel Wars* (Bozeman, MT: End Time Thunder Publishers, 2011), 249.
215.   Dr. Michael Lake, *The Shinar Directive* (Crane, MO: Defender, 2014), 63; 218.

216.   Stephen Quayle, *Angel Wars* (Bozeman, MT: End Time Thunder Publishers, 2011), 288.

217.   Stephen Quayle, *Terminated* (Bozeman, MT: End Time Thunder Publishers, 2018), 109; 158.

218.   Cris Putnam & Thomas Horn, *Exo-Vaticana* (Crane, MO: Defender, 2013), 120.

219.   Ibid., pp. 120-121.

220.   Leon R. Kass, *Life, Liberty, and the Defense of Dignity: the Challenge for Bioethics* (New York, NY: Encounter, 2002), introduction.

221.   *Pandemonium's Engine*, Thomas Horn, D.D., "Pandemonium and 'Her' Children," p. 31 (Crane, MO: Defender, 2011).

222.   Stephen Quayle, *Terminated* (Bozeman, MT: End Time Thunder Publishers, 2018), 108.

223.   Ibid., p. 159.

224.   Paul McGuire & Troy Anderson, *The Babylon Code* (NY, NY: *Faith Words*, Hachette Book Group, 2015), 271.

225.   Stephen Quayle, *Angel Wars* (Bozeman, MT: End Time Thunder Publishers, 2011), 282.

226.   Stephen Quayle, *Terminated* (Bozeman, MT: End Time Thunder Publishers, 2018), 163.

227.   Ibid., p. 116.

228.   Ibid., p. 214.

229.   Stephen Quayle, *Angel Wars* (Bozeman, MT: End Time Thunder Publishers, 2011), 343.

230.   Ibid., p. 283.

231.   Cris Putnam & Thomas Horn, *Exo-Vaticana* (Crane, MO: Defender, 2013), 119.

232.   Stephen Quayle, *Angel Wars* (Bozeman, MT: End Time Thunder Publishers, 2011), 255-256.

233.   *Pandemonium's Engine*, John P. McTernan, Ph.D., Genetic Armageddon, p. 266 (Crane, MO: Defender, 2011).

234.   Stephen Quayle, *Terminated* (Bozeman, MT: End Time Thunder Publishers, 2018), 169.

235.   Ibid., p. 129.

236.   Stephen Quayle, *Angel Wars* (Bozeman, MT: End Time Thunder Publishers, 2011), 233-234.

237.   *Pandemonium's Engine*, Douglas Hamp, "Man Becoming His Own God?." p. 238 (Crane, MO: Defender, 2011).

238.   Stephen Quayle & Dr. Thomas R. Horn, *Unearthing the Lost World of the Cloudeaters* (Crane, MO: Defender, 2017), 197.

239.   Ibid., p. 195.

240.   Stephen Quayle, *Angel Wars* (Bozeman, MT: End Time Thunder Publishers, 2011), 270.

241.   Stephen Quayle, *Terminated* (Bozeman, MT: End Time Thunder Publishers, 2018), 195.

242.   Stephen Quayle, *Angel Wars* (Bozeman, MT: End Time Thunder Publishers, 2011), 272.

243.   Stephen Quayle, *Terminated* (Bozeman, MT: End Time Thunder Publishers, 2018), 16.

244.   Ibid.

245.   Gary Stearman, "Prophecy and the Human Genome," *Prophecy in the News* (June 2014) p. 9.

246.   Stephen Quayle, *Terminated* (Bozeman, MT: End Time Thunder Publishers, 2018), 17.

247.   Ibid., p. 18.

248.   Ibid., pp. 18-19.

249.   Ibid., p. 19.

250.   Ibid., p. 198.

251.   Ibid., p. 232.

252.   Ibid., pp. 298-299.

253.   https://en.wikipedia.org/wiki/Neanderthal_genetics.

254.   Gary Stearman, "The Twisted History of the Genetic War," *Prophecy Watcher* (October 2019), p. 6.

255.   Stephen Quayle & Dr. Thomas R. Horn, *Unearthing the Lost World of the Cloudeaters* (Crane, MO: Defender, 2017), 91-92.

256.   Cris Putnam & Thomas Horn, *Exo-Vaticana* (Crane, MO: Defender, 2013) 317.

257.   Stephen Quayle, *Angel Wars* (Bozeman, MT: End Time Thunder Publishers, 2011), 292.

258.   Cris Putnam & Thomas Horn, *Exo-Vaticana* (Crane, MO: Defender, 2013) 202-203.

259.   L.A Marzulli, "Cattle Mutilations," *Prophecy Watcher*, p. 36, (March 2019).

260.   Stephen Quayle & Dr. Thomas R. Horn, *Unearthing the Lost World of the Cloudeaters* (Crane, MO: Defender, 2017), 203-204.

261.   Ibid., p. 202.

262.   Stephen Quayle, *Angel Wars* (Bozeman, MT: End Time Thunder Publishers, 2011), 193.

263.   Ibid., p. 194.

264.   Ibid.

265.   Ibid.

266.   Ibid., p. 195.

267.   Cris Putnam & Thomas Horn, *Exo-Vaticana* (Crane, MO: Defender, 2013), 211.

268.   Ibid., p. 123.

269.   Steve Schmutzer, "Who are the Sons of God in Genesis 6," p. 28, *Prophecy Watcher*, (February 2019).

270.   Cris Putnam & Thomas Horn, *Exo-Vaticana* (Crane, MO: Defender, 2013), 123.

271.   Ibid., p. 228.

272.   "Satan's Counterfeits: Judgment Day UFOs, Angels & End Time Prophecy," mt.net/~watcher, 2003.

273.   Stephen Quayle & Dr. Thomas R. Horn, *Unearthing the Lost World of the Cloudeaters* (Crane, MO: Defender, 2017), 231.

274.   Cris Putnam & Thomas Horn, *Exo-Vaticana* (Crane, MO: Defender, 2013), 316.

275.   Stephen Quayle & Dr. Thomas R. Horn, *Unearthing the Lost World of the Cloudeaters* (Crane, MO: Defender, 2017), 160.

276.   Ibid., pp. 128-129.

277.   Ibid., p.151.

278.   Ibid., pp. 135; 142.

279.   Ibid., p. 135.

280.   www.ancientpages.com/2014/11/19/mystery-lost-underground-city-grand-canyon.

281.   Stephen Quayle & Dr. Thomas R.
Horn, *Unearthing the Lost World of the
Cloudeaters* (Crane, MO: Defender, 2017), 73-
73.

282.   *Pandemonium's Engine*, Cris D.
Putnam, "Christian Transhumanism:
Pandemonium's Latest Ploy," p. 198, (Crane,
MO: Defender, 2011).

283.   Stephen Quayle, *Angel Wars*
(Bozeman, MT: End Time Thunder
Publishers, 2011), 332.

284.   Ibid., p. 336.

285.   Stephen Quayle & Dr. Thomas R.
Horn, *Unearthing the Lost World of the
Cloudeaters* (Crane, MO: Defender, 2017),
167.

286.   Ibid., p. 168.

287.   Ibid., p. 186.

288.   Ibid., p. 188.

289.   Ibid., p. 170.

290.   Ibid., p. 191.

291.   Cris Putnam & Thomas Horn, *Exo-
Vaticana* (Crane, MO: Defender, 2013), 20.

292.   Ibid., 38.

293.   Stephen Quayle & Dr. Thomas R.
Horn, *Unearthing the Lost World of the
Cloudeaters* (Crane, MO: Defender, 2017),
143-146; 408-411.

294.   Cris Putnam & Thomas Horn, *Exo-Vaticana* (Crane, MO: Defender, 2013), 22.

295.   Ibid., p. 23.

296.   Ibid., p. 19.

297.   Ibid., p. 176.

298.   Ibid., p. 209.

www.ingramcontent.com/pod-product-compliance
Lightning Source LLC
Chambersburg PA
CBHW071525040426
42452CB00008B/885